Christian Miracles

AMAZING STORIES OF
GOD'S HELPING HAND
IN OUR EVERYDAY LIVES

James S. Bell
&
Stephen R. Clark

ADAMS MEDIA
Avon, Massachusetts

Copyright ©2005 F+W Publications, Inc.
All rights reserved. This book, or parts thereof, may not be reproduced
in any form without permission from the publisher; exceptions
are made for brief excerpts used in published reviews.

Published by
Adams Media, an F+W Publications Company
57 Littlefield Street, Avon, MA 02322. U.S.A.
www.adamsmedia.com

ISBN: 1-59337-271-X

Printed in Canada.

J I H G F E D C B A

Library of Congress Cataloging-in-Publication Data
Bell, James S.
Christian miracles / James S. Bell and Stephen R. Clark.
p.   cm.
ISBN 1-59337-271-X
1. Miracles—Anecdotes. 2. Christian life—Anecdotes. I. Clark, Stephen R. II. Title.
BT97.3.B45 2005
231.7'3—dc22
2004026014

This publication is designed to provide accurate and authoritative information with
regard to the subject matter covered. It is sold with the understanding that the publisher is not engaged in rendering legal, accounting, or other professional advice.
If legal advice or other expert assistance is required, the services of a competent professional person should be sought.
　　—From a *Declaration of Principles* jointly adopted by a Committee of the Ameri-
　　　can Bar Association and a Committee of Publishers and Associations

Many of the designations used by manufacturers and sellers to distinguish their prod-
ucts are claimed as trademarks. Where those designations appear in this book and
Adams Media was aware of a trademark claim, the designations have been printed
with initial capital letters.

While all the events and experiences recounted in this book are true and happened to
real people, some of the names, dates, and places have been changed in order to protect
the privacy of certain individuals.

Interior Photograph © 2001 Brand X Pictures.

This book is available at quantity discounts for bulk purchases.
For information, please call 1-800-872-5627.

To my two sons-in-law, Andrew Burdett and
Noah Ritchie, the "miracles" in our daughters' lives.
May your faith in God's power grow as you lead the way.
—*Jim*

To my parents, Walter and Grace Clark,
and their legacy of faith, which is being passed on
through me, my sister, our families, and beyond.
—*Stephen*

Acknowledgments

WE WISH TO THANK the dozens of people who submitted hundreds of stories as we assembled this book. While we were unable to use them all, each story brought its own special blessing. Even though some stories didn't quite fit in the category of a miracle, it is a delight to know that those sharing them clearly experienced God's intervention in their situation, as comforter, provider, and Lord. A special thanks goes to Kate Epstein and Bridget Brace, as well as others behind the scenes at Adams Media, who have exercised sensitive stewardship over this project. And, above all, we give thanks to God, Who was the cause behind each miracle reported herein, and Who preserved the manuscript through two hard-drive crashes. That this book came to fruition is evidence that God cares about us in the big things as well as the lesser things in our lives.

Foreword

WHAT DO YOU THINK OF TODAY when you think of a miracle? For some of us, it's the birth of a baby. For others it may be the Chicago Cubs winning the World Series. But the older, original meaning of this word gives it a higher source: "an act or happening attributed to supernatural power." In simple terms, a miracle is a happening that neither human beings nor nature is capable of causing—God Himself has to step in and give us a helping hand. The events just mentioned may be marvelous, but they're not truly miracles.

It's understandable that we often associate divine miracles with great events, like God parting the Red Sea for the Israelites or Jesus raising Lazarus from the dead. Yet God isn't just concerned with extraordinary displays of power or working only with biblical superstars. He cares deeply about ordinary people like you and me. Sometimes He lets us struggle to deepen our character. But at other times He intervenes in ways that go beyond our capacity and the laws of nature. Why? Well, being God, He has the power, and sometimes His purposes won't come about in any other way.

This book is all about the times when God intervenes and dramatically changes things for our good, because He loves us and wants the best for us. When we face danger, have financial needs, are sick, or desperately need guidance, most of the time God works in mysterious, quiet, and natural ways to help us. But sometimes things happen that make us scratch our heads and say the only explanation is a miracle.

The presence and power of the supernatural—that is, the Father; his son, Jesus; and the Holy Spirit—within the ordinary events of life are heavenly reminders that He cares about both the little things and the big things we face every day. He may miraculously save the life of one person, but He may also provide an astounding way for another to pay his gas bill. We can't limit or figure out God, but it is inspiring to read about His great variety of exploits on behalf of ordinary people with whom we can identify.

Hopefully, this book will draw you closer to God as you see Him reveal Himself in dramatic and unexpected ways. One of these stories might even jog your memory, and maybe you'll recall something similar from your own past—something that now convinces you God was present then, in a way you may not have realized at the time. This understanding may make you appreciate Him more and even strengthen your faith that, if necessary, He may do something similar for you when you need it. Sometimes we don't even need it, but God, in the abundance of His love, gives us a miracle anyway.

Miracles didn't cease when Jesus and his apostles left this earth. God promised to be with us always and to be active on our behalf. As you'll find, prayer and simple faith can sometimes trigger His response in unusual ways. At the least, you can be sure He'll never leave you or forsake you. He shares in all your joys and sorrows. So be encouraged, and may this book be a tiny miracle in your own life.

*S*teven Manchester was a sergeant E-5, squad leader and military policeman in the U.S. Army during Operation Desert Shield and Operation Desert Storm in Iraq. Two weeks after the liberation of Kuwait, Steven was standing guard at a barren traffic control point when a lone vehicle approached. It belonged to an American, so he waved it through. The driver pulled up to him and stopped. He was lost.

"Man, am I glad to see you!" the driver said to Steven with a nervous grin. "I lost my convoy in the sandstorm that just passed through. I'm supposed to be on Main Supply Route Green, but I don't think I am."

"You're not that far off," Steven assured him. "Right now, you're on M.S.R. Blue, but this route runs parallel to M.S.R. Green. Keep south for the next four miles or so, and when you reach a fork in the road, you've met up with Green."

The sergeant's face showed relief and with a wave, he was on his way.

One afternoon in base camp, several months later, Steven's platoon sergeant, Tony Rosini, approached. "Hey, kid, got any plans today?" They both had the day off.

"Yeah, I think I'll head to the mall," Steven joked.

Tony chuckled. "In that case, you can give me a ride into Saudi Arabia. My knee has been acting up, so maybe they'll give me some painkillers. Either way, I could use the time away, and from the looks of it, so could you."

Steven and Tony jumped into a Humvee and headed off, with Steven driving. They traveled down the dusty roads at a fast clip, making good time, joking and laughing. There were only forty miles between them and the Saudi Arabian border.

Before long they were out of communications range, and radio traffic ceased. Steven noticed that they hadn't seen any other vehicles on the road since they left. Both continually scanned the vast terrain to make sure they really were alone.

Several miles passed, and a bad sandstorm began to blow. In the blink of an eye, the blue sky had turned a blinding orange as the harsh winds of the open desert rearranged the landscape. Steven had to slow almost to a stop. He could barely see three feet past the windshield.

With just thirty miles left to the border, there was a sudden, loud bang from the right side of the Humvee. In what seemed like super-slow motion, the vehicle tipped left, toward the driver's side. Cracks spider-webbed the windshield. The desert spun; an Army field phone struck Steven in the back of his head, and he went limp.

"I felt as if I were submerged into a pool of warm water," says Steven. "Unlike any peace I had ever experienced before, the sensation was heavenly. With no choice but to accept the comfort, my eyes slammed shut. In the briefest moment in time, I watched as my life played out before me. It was a slide show, with one vivid picture after another being brought into the light."

Then Steven began to regain consciousness. His entire body throbbed, and he noticed his wedding band had been knocked off his finger. He could see the Humvee—forty feet away, upside down with the engine still running, wheels spinning aimlessly.

With all of his strength, Steven pushed himself to his knees and moved slowly toward the wreck. Tony was still inside, suspended upside down by his seatbelt and out cold. Focusing all of his energy, Steven reached into the Humvee and got Tony loose. He pulled Tony free of the wreckage, unsure if his friend was even still alive, and moved away from the overturned vehicle.

A safe distance away, Steven laid Tony onto the warm sand and checked his pulse. He was alive. "Feeling the greatest sense of relief, I was promptly reacquainted with my own pain," says Steven. "The intensity of it made me nauseous. I felt as if I were going to pass out as Tony was waking up."

The Humvee gave one final whine and then went still. Steven sat in the sand with Tony's head in his lap. Tony was in shock and mumbling gibberish. Steven treated him as best he could and tried to reassure him. "Don't you worry, Tony. I'll get us out of this one. We'll be okay." But Steven wasn't so sure.

Steven decided to try the radio in the Humvee. Approaching the smoking wreckage, he saw what had caused the accident. Blinded by the sandstorm, they had veered off the roadway and hit a boulder, which caused the Humvee to flip. The driver's side, where Steven had been, was completely crushed and the door had been ripped off.

Had Steven been wearing his seatbelt, he would have been trapped inside and crushed in the vehicle. He had also not been wearing his helmet, which is why he was knocked out by the phone. Unconscious and limp, unbuckled, and undeterred by a door, Steven had actually been tossed to safety onto the sand. It was a miracle in the midst of disaster.

Steven got to the radio, but the antenna was buried in the sand, rendering it useless. Still, he tried repeatedly to contact someone. There was no food and only a little water. They weren't expected back in camp for at least twenty-four hours, so until then no one would come looking for them.

Fighting off despair, Steven grabbed his rifle, a box of ammo, and a ragged blanket, and returned to Tony. The only things left were faith and hope, and "I felt I was losing both at the time," says Steven.

Hours must have passed; Tony became more coherent. "What the heck happened?" he asked. Steven explained their circumstances and expressed his concern. "You worry too much, Stevie-boy. Just get us the heck out of here!"

Steven smiled and then lied, "No sweat, boss. I made the call. Help should be here in no time." Tony said nothing; he just grinned weakly as he lapsed back into unconsciousness. All Steven could do was wait and pray. He was "praying like you can't believe," Steven says now.

Steven felt a good bit of despair, despite his faith in Christ. They had no way to call for help, and the chances of someone driving past were extremely remote. With each passing minute, the outcome looked more and more bleak. Tony was in and out of consciousness and getting worse. For the first time since the war started, Steven cried. Then, their angel appeared.

An American vehicle materialized on the horizon. Soon, a man's hand rested on Steven's shoulder. Looking up, Steven couldn't believe his eyes. It was the same lost sergeant Steven had helped several months earlier. Smiling, Steven said, "Man, am I glad to see you! But how did you find us?"

The sergeant said, "I'm going to take care of you now. It's all over. We'll get you out of here." With that, he winked and then looked back at the road. "I'm assigned to the scout vehicle with my medical unit. I'm about ten minutes ahead of our convoy. They should be along in a bit."

"So how did you know we were here?" Steven asked again. "Did you hear my radio transmission?"

"What transmission? We were just passing through."

In a mixture of amazement, pain, and relief, Steven collapsed. The angel, Sergeant Jason Matthews, a medic, called for a chopper, and then went to work treating both men and caring for their injuries. They were then airlifted to safety.

As Steven was being taken to the helicopter, Sergeant Matthews pressed something into his hand. Then, with a wonderful smile and a thumbs-up, the medic was gone.

Steven opened his hand and there was his gold wedding band, slightly misshapen, but shining brightly.

"I had lived through it. I slid the ring back onto my finger, and the chopper took to the air. Miraculously, Tony and I were both healed. I stayed in the army until the Gulf War ended. Tony retired with a disability from the army, and to this day, still offers to pay for driving lessons for me. Most important, the ordeal has confirmed my faith in God and Christ ever since."

Steven was honorably discharged from the army in 1991 upon returning home from Operation Desert Storm.

One pleasant spring day in 2001, Lura Maiman was driving along a treacherous two-lane mountain highway in Israel, where she lived with her husband Milt. One side of the road was buttressed by a wall of rock, and the other fell away to a sheer dropoff.

Her fellow drivers showed no caution—despite the numerous warning signs and a solid no-passing line, cars would still pass one another on hills and blind curves, sometimes several at a time. Even when drivers could see cars ahead of them, they often refused to yield the right of way, forcing a dangerous game of chicken for those coming toward them.

Lura suddenly and scarily found herself in just that situation. She rounded a curve with the forbidding rock wall to her right and a line of cars in the other lane. Coming toward her, in her lane—attempting to pass the other cars—were not one, but *two* cars squeezed side by side.

She had no room to swerve, and the oncoming cars made no attempt to slow down or maneuver to avoid her. They were locked in a battle with each other and seemed not to even see Lura's car.

The cars sped toward her, and at that moment she merely assumed her time for a Heavenly Homegoing had arrived. She closed her eyes and calmly prayed, "Lord, it is in Your Hands. I commit my spirit to You." Then she braced herself for the crash.

Several seconds passed, and nothing happened. She felt no impact. She heard no rush of cars. She cautiously opened her eyes. There were no cars in front of her in her lane. Looking into her rearview mirror, she could see the same two cars still locked in a deadly race down the highway in the wrong lane, with the line of cars still flowing through the opposite lane.

What had happened? Lura could think of only one nearly unbelievable, yet supremely glorious explanation: God had performed a miracle, somehow taking those cars through hers or hers through theirs, sparing her life. She continued on home, praising the Lord for such an amazing miracle, eager to share the story with Milt.

After thirty-five years of marriage, Milt died from a pneumonia-like illness. Lura remained in Israel and remarried. Today, Lura and her husband, Eddie Beckford, run a chess club and book shop in the city of Arad, working with the Russian immigrants there. They make Christian books available free for anyone who wants them.

—as told by Susan Heagy, Lura's sister

While she was a student at Fuller Theological Seminary, Sybil Clark helped lead a support group for sexually abused women. During a meeting of the group, one of the women requested prayer. She had suffered from internal abdominal problems and was on a number of medications. Recently, tests had indicated two large growths in her intestines, and she was going in for surgery.

"Of course we were all very willing to pray for her," says Sybil. "There were about six of us there. She lay down on a couch and each woman prayed in turn. While the others were praying I had a vision of the Holy Spirit moving through the woman's body, touching the trouble spots. When my turn came to pray, I prayed exactly what I had envisioned."

While Sybil was praying, the woman rested her hands on the areas above each of the growths, which she could feel. As soon as Sybil finished praying, the woman shared what had just taken place.

Sybil recalls, "She felt a cool breeze moving through her body exactly as I was praying would happen. As I prayed, she could feel each growth, in turn, move. She asked me if she had been healed. I told her she needed to go to the hospital and let the doctors determine that."

The woman went in for her surgery on the following Thursday. Early Friday morning, she called Sybil and reported what had happened. The doctor, who was also a Christian, spent five hours doing exploratory surgery. He told her he could find no trace of the growths. There was no unhealthy tissue anywhere. He said that whatever had been there was gone. He then instructed her to go home and throw out all of the medications he had given her because she was now a healthy woman.

When Harold (Hal) J. Oppenhuis accepted Christ as his Savior, he was thirty-seven years old. In the summer of 1973 Hal read the entire Bible, from Genesis to Revelation, in ten days. He says, "I was set on fire for things of God. Even before I was saved I was hungry."

However, Hal could not stop smoking cigarettes. "I had everyone pray for me, and I was given all sorts of ideas, like I should lay my cigarettes on the altar and just walk away. I'd go home from church and have a cigarette. I could not quit, even though I wanted to. I finally thought I would be a smoking Christian forever." Hal never stopped praying.

Ironically, Hal was a health teacher. One January day in 1974, Hal was teaching his students about how smoking affects the lungs. One student asked him, "Mr. Oppenhuis, don't *you* smoke?"

Of course, Hal had to say yes. But then something very odd began to happen to him.

"I felt an intense burning in my chest for about fifteen to twenty seconds. I couldn't move. That something happened was obvious even to the thirty students in the classroom. After that feeling passed, I never had another cigarette. Even the desire was gone. Jesus, my Lord and Savior, had miraculously delivered me from smoking as I stood there in class!"

About a month later, during that same class, a student asked Hal what happened that day. The room got very quiet—everyone wanted to hear. "I told them that the Lord had taken away my addiction to smoking."

Every time Hal tells someone about that miracle moment, he feels a warm tingling sensation in his chest. Today, Hal leads a Bible study in Indianapolis, Indiana, for recovering alcoholics and drug addicts. "I know that God can take away addictions instantly. God has given me real faith in this area to pray for these people. I would not walk another day without Jesus."

*B*ob and Judy Lambert regularly took their oldest grandson, Dylan, to church with them. Even though there were separate classes for the kids, Dylan preferred to sit in the service with his grandparents. Dylan had been diagnosed with asthma at only eight months old.

One night, when Dylan was five and a half years old, he woke up in the early hours gasping for breath. His breathing machine and inhalers were not with him at his grandparents' house. Bob was at work, and Judy didn't have a car.

Judy called her daughter, Michelle. She told Michelle that Dylan was having problems breathing and asked her to rush over with his machine and medicines. Judy then carried Dylan into the living room to anxiously wait for his mother.

"I realized that he could die before his mother got there," recalls Judy. "I held him and told him, 'Dylan, Mammy is going to pray healing for you.' And that's what I did! When I was finished praying, Dylan came up off the couch and gasped out, 'Mammy, it may not sound like it, but I'm healed!' Then he marched up and down the hallway with his little arms in the air praising Jesus and thanking him for his healing. Each breath came clearer and deeper. When his mother came running in with his breathing machine he told her he was healed," says Judy proudly.

When Dylan was just seven years old, he was prayed over, and someone prophesied that he would be used mightily of God. Evidence of this came only a few weeks later.

Judy watched Dylan and his baby brother, Jordan, while their mom was at work. Judy and the two boys had just returned home from a trip to the library when her phone rang. "It was my daughter," says Judy. "She was at the police station. A man she was supposed to be showing an apartment to had attacked her and held her for over half an hour. Despite the man's efforts, my daughter was unhurt. I told her that Bob would be right there to pick her up.

"The boys knew something was wrong," explains Judy. "I told them that a bad man had tried to hurt their mother, but that she was okay. And I said we should pray for her. After I had prayed thanking the Lord for protecting her, Dylan asked if he could pray. 'Of course!' I told him. All he said was, 'Jesus help my daddy not to hurt that bad man.' To this point I had not even thought of that possibility."

Michelle's escape had been miraculous. The man began his attack on the third floor of the apartment building. He then tried to force Michelle down the stairs and into the basement of the building. They got to the ground floor and began to struggle in front of a glass window door. Simultaneously, a woman named Linda, who was a meter maid and who attended the same church as Michelle and Judy, drove by in her car. (That day, Linda just happened to be working an extra shift.) As she drove by, she looked in her rearview mirror and caught a glimpse of the man, who had nothing but his underwear on, and Michelle's face through the glass door. Linda whipped her car around and jumped out. This provided the distraction Michelle needed and she broke free. Michelle went straight to her husband, John, before going to the police.

An angry and distraught John immediately headed for the building. He swore he would kill the man if he found him. When the police arrived on the scene, however, John had the man pinned on the ground, and had not hurt him.

Says Michelle, "John shared that he had his fist poised to bash the man's face, but suddenly he couldn't move his arm. A little boy's prophetic prayer had helped his daddy do the right thing."

The family knows that God will always watch over their two boys. In June of 2004, Bob, John, Dylan, now eighteen, and Jordan, eleven, headed out for a fishing trip to Canada. They flew deep into the woods and planned to go canoeing from there. One evening as they set up camp, Jordan, showing a boy's impulsive eagerness, headed up a trail alone. Bob was watching him and started to head after his grandson. But John and Dylan had accidentally tipped their canoe just before getting to the shore. They fell into the water with all of their supplies. Bob's focus quickly shifted to the immediate need to help gather up everything, including their maps, before it floated away. In the meantime, Jordan continued on the trail, oblivious to the fact that he was utterly alone.

A while later, Jordan realized he was lost. Scared, he stopped walking and called for his dad, but there was no reply. His proximity to thundering rapids helped muffle his small voice. Jordan began to cry. But Jordan knew God. In his fear, he asked God what he should do. "God spoke to me and told me to climb up on a big rock that was right in front of me," states Jordan. That's exactly what he did.

When he reached the top of the rock, Jordan saw the path that led back to camp. He jumped down and ran along it until he saw the rest of his family. Today, Jordan and Dylan both know that God helps them in whatever situation that comes along. They've experienced miracles both big and small.

*J*ean Graham's evangelical Christian upbringing had given her a firm belief in angels, agents of the most high God, sent as protectors and defenders of His children.

On a dark street in 1987, something occurred that had never happened to her before, and hasn't since.

After teaching a writers' workshop, Jean was driving through the quiet residential streets of East San Diego. It was after 10:00 P.M., and, anxious to get home, Jean was pushing the speed limit. As she sped toward an intersection where she had the right of way, she heard a voice.

"It was in clear, precise English," says Jean, "in a tone that was somehow neither male nor female, but full of a commanding urgency that definitely conveyed a warning."

The voice said, "Slow down to the speed limit."

Startled, Jean lightened her touch on the gas pedal and at the same instant heard the wail of a siren approaching fast. Just as she entered the intersection, a small red sports car crossed in front of her, running the stop sign at about eighty miles per hour. Right behind the red car was a police car in hot pursuit.

"I hit my brakes and skidded to a stunned stop just after they had cleared the intersection," says Jean. "And they were gone! The whole episode from when I heard the voice to when I stopped was no more than a few seconds."

As she sat in her car, shaking a bit, she recalled a verse from the Bible that her mother had taught when she had been scared as a child: "For the angel of the Lord guards all who fear him, and he rescues them" (Ps. 34:7).

"So on that dark street," says Jean, "I imagined those same angels surrounding my car, faithfully keeping me out of harm's way. I stopped shaking then, touched the accelerator, and confidently headed for home, in awe of the miracle God had just provided."

*I*t would be easy for Lisa Faul to blame the lack of a Christian upbringing for her behavior. She could even point to an absentee father and a dysfunctional family and say they caused it. But she knows that it was the love of alcohol and immoral behavior during her teen years that quickly propelled her life into a dark abyss from which she thought she would never climb out.

When Lisa was eight years old, a playmate told her about the fun things she did at church. Since Lisa felt there was no fun in her own life, she invited herself to attend church with her friend. It was there that Lisa heard about God for the first time.

At nearly the same time, Lisa became curious about the wine her mother drank. She reasoned that it must taste pretty good because her mother drank it so often. Lisa began taking sips of wine when her mother wasn't looking, and she fell in love with it.

By age fifteen, Lisa and a girlfriend routinely left their homes on Saturday nights and crossed the nearby border into Mexico. There, feeling very mature in their mini-skirts and black fishnet stockings, they drank until they were drunk. Lisa loved everything about alcohol—the way it tasted, the way it made her feel, and the power she thought it gave her.

They would stumble back to the girlfriend's house late each Saturday night. Every Sunday morning, her girlfriend's father would wake them and insist they go to church with him. Says Lisa, "Although they were aware that we had been out all night drinking, the members of the little church turned a blind eye to our appearance and the alcohol on our breath. Instead, they chose to love us anyway and encouraged us to continue coming."

The pastor would often say to Lisa, "Lisa, do you want to talk? How can we help you? Are you ready to stop drinking?"

Lisa wasn't ready to stop, but she felt guilty because of how kind the pastor was despite her condition. "Even when I was reeling from a hangover," says Lisa, "God spoke to me through the sermons. No matter where I was, no matter my condition, Jesus continued knocking on the door of my heart—wanting me to come to Him." Just as Lisa would not let go of the alcohol she had become addicted to at age eight, the God she had also encountered that year would not let go of her.

"A tubal pregnancy at fifteen ended with the loss of my unborn child," says Lisa, "and nearly took my life as well. In the years to come, this pregnancy would affect all efforts to become pregnant."

During her few sober times, Lisa would try to take a good look at her miserable existence. "God, my life isn't supposed to look like this," she would cry out. "Why is this happening? What do you want from me?" But even as she wondered if she would ever be free from the powerful, dark forces controlling her life, she continued drinking and also began abusing drugs.

In 1992, at the age of twenty-four, Lisa hit bottom. "In addition to everything else, I was now homeless. Although embarrassed and ashamed of my condition, with no place else to go, I moved in with my father, who had become a part of my life. I somehow managed to stop drinking for one year, but with my poor choice of friends, sobriety did not last long."

But God was still pursuing her. Gary, a frequent customer where Lisa worked, somehow seemed to recognize her struggle and made a point to encourage her each time he saw her. He would tell Lisa, "Take it one day at a time.

Look to God for your strength. You can do it. God can help you."

Lisa didn't realize until later that those words were what Gary heard at his Alcoholics Anonymous meetings. Having been where she was, he knew what she was going through.

One day, Gary gently confronted her, "Lisa, you look horrible. You just can't go on like this. Let me pick you up this evening after work and take you someplace where you can get help." Amazingly, with no idea what he meant or where they would go, Lisa agreed.

Gary took Lisa to the Alona Club, a meeting place for recovering alcoholics. That night, she became determined to finally get sober and stay sober. Step one was to attend those meetings on a regular basis.

"Shortly after that first meeting," says Lisa, "I was transferred to the late-night shift at work. That meant I was at work while the bars were open. I truly believe it was God who rearranged my schedule to put that temptation even farther from me."

After a year of encouragement from Alona Club meetings, Lisa finally began seeking God with all her heart. "From my first introduction to God, I never doubted His existence and never stopped talking to Him. I had asked Jesus to be my Savior in the past. Now I was asking from my heart. I had no idea what the future would hold, but was certain He was real and that His hand was on my life."

Today, Lisa is a living example of 2 Corinthians 5:17: "Therefore, if anyone is in Christ, he is a new creation; the old has gone, the new has come" (NIV).

"From all I've experienced," she says, "I should be dead by now. But instead I've been given a new life—a life of sobriety for more than eleven years. During this time, I have experienced God's miraculous work in my life over and over."

—as told to Joanne Schulte by Lisa Faul

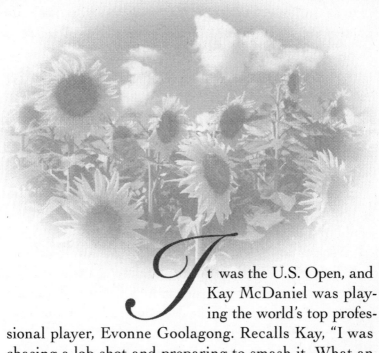

*I*t was the U.S. Open, and Kay McDaniel was playing the world's top professional player, Evonne Goolagong. Recalls Kay, "I was chasing a lob shot and preparing to smash it. What an exhilarating feeling to catapult in the air, extending every muscle, and exert maximum energy just to hit a fluffy tennis ball." But she had pushed her body too far. She developed a bone spur that wouldn't go away. It completely halted her career.

"As a professional tennis player, I relied upon my body to perform extraordinary feats, for it was my passport to success. Daily, I buffeted it to make it stronger than the day before, ignoring any pain along the way. Will I ever play again?" she wondered. Kay took herself out of tournament play indefinitely and opted for surgery. It was successful, but three weeks afterward, she felt the exact same pain as before surgery. Her career was over at the ripe old age of twenty-three.

"Then the extraordinary happened," explains Kay. "One night, the television was on in the background when I heard a man blurt out from the screen, 'There is a young lady with a bone spur on her left heel and God is going to heal you.' Shaking, I dropped to my knees, tears streaming from my face, and I tilted my head to heaven, 'Oh God, could You do this for me, would You heal me?'"

Weeks passed. Then one morning Kay awoke with no pain in her foot. "I rushed to the tennis court where it had all begun, where I first learned to hit a tennis ball. I tested my foot. Truly, God had healed my heel! I whipped my body back into playing shape, and three months later I returned to the tour, traveling the world again."

Kay played six years on the professional tour. Her first U.S. Open was in 1980; her last, in 1986. She also played Wimbledon six times and was ranked in the top thirty in the world in singles, and in the top twenty in doubles.

*B*etty King's daughter, Melody, and her husband were having financial problems. Her husband was losing his business, and things were rough. "I didn't know, though, how bad their troubles had actually become," says Betty. "Melody had walked quietly through valleys before in her life. I had failed to realize the extent of her worries on previous occasions."

Because Betty suffered from multiple sclerosis, Melody didn't want to upset her, so she chose not to tell her mother just how bad things were for her and her husband. Melody's second son was born when her first was not quite two years old. They lived just down the street from Betty, who rode her three-wheel, motorized scooter down the block to visit Melody and the grandkids almost every day.

Betty says, "I talked daily with my daughter, yet I was still unaware of her extreme difficulties. I knew money was sparse; I didn't know there was none."

One day, while cleaning a closet, Betty came across a jumbo package of baby diapers left over from one of her other grandchildren. She decided Melody could probably use them. She picked up the phone and called her daughter. "Melody, I found a big package of diapers in the closet; could you use them for Frankie?"

"Yes, Mom—I'll be right down to get them!" Melody seemed awfully excited about a silly package of diapers, Betty thought.

It wasn't until years later that Melody explained to her mother what a miracle those diapers had been. She said, "I had just put the last diaper on Frankie and didn't have money to buy any more."

Melody remembered what the Bible said about having the faith of a little child. "So I prayed: Lord, that was my last diaper. I don't have money to buy any more. Please send me some diapers for my baby."

In her childlike faith, Melody truly expected to open her front door and find some diapers sitting on her front porch. "But instead the phone rang, Mom, and it was you!"

Her prayer had been answered at just the right time with exactly what she needed.

*E*mmarie and Eddie Lehnick's six-year-old daughter Debbie was a chronic asthmatic. She had spent much of her short life in and out of the hospital. Many times when an asthma attack hit, she would dehydrate quickly and go into shock. "With each attack," explains Emmarie, "we felt sheer panic. We would rush her to the hospital, which was twenty miles away. Immediately, she would be given cortisone, oxygen, antibiotic, and an IV. This was the routine asthma treatment at the time. We nearly lost her twice when she went into shock."

The doctors tested Debbie for allergies and determined that she should get two allergy shots a week. For the young girl, just knowing and dreading the day of the shots could trigger an asthma attack. Her parents were able to control food allergies, but molds, pollens, and weather fronts often triggered the allergic response in Debbie. Emmarie says she became obsessive in her protection of her daughter.

One afternoon, Emmarie and Eddie planned a trip to the small town of Lefors, fifty miles away, where they had previously taught and made close friends. Emmarie was nervous about taking her daughter on such a long trip, and she repeatedly questioned her husband about it.

"Should we risk taking Debbie to the Lefors vespers service?"

"The weather is good, and vespers will not last long," Eddie said, attempting to allay Emmarie's anxiety. The family climbed into their blue and white '56 Pontiac and headed out. It was a clear day with only a few white fluffy clouds dotting the sky.

"Would you look at that?" said Eddie pointing toward a hilltop they were approaching. "It's a tremendous rainbow. I guess Lefors got some rain."

When they got to the top of the hill, Eddie pulled over to the shoulder of the road. They could barely believe what they were experiencing. "It was like we were actually at the end of the rainbow," says Emmarie. "The bright bands of color reached across the sky like a giant protractor, and each band seemed to be at least eight feet wide. It was enormous from the first color to the last. We jumped out of the car and began running and leaping in the wide bands of the rainbow ribbon, which puddled on the road to about half the length of a football field."

"Look at me," exclaimed Debbie, "I'm purple!"

"I'm red!" shrieked her brother Mark.

"Amazingly, there was no sign of rain anywhere around us," recalls Emmarie, "There was not even the smell of rain in the air. We joined hands in a circle and danced in God's rainbow. I felt like a child again as I frolicked in the hues, spinning and turning and lifting my arms to catch the colors."

"In Sunday School, we learned Noah saw the rainbow," Debbie informed her family.

Eddie lifted Mark onto the rainbow-drenched hood of the car. "That's right. The rainbow is God's promise that never again will all life be destroyed by a flood."

"I'll bet this is how Joseph felt in his coat of many colors," said Debbie as she skipped across the pavement.

"Some stories have a pot of gold at the end of the rainbow. My pot of gold is here," Emmarie affirmed as she hugged her children. "I have never seen anything this wonderful. I feel like God has wrapped us in His rainbow of love. I just know this is a blessing from Him. How many people get to dance in an enormous rainbow? This is awesome. I think we should thank God for this heavenly moment."

Eddie lifted Debbie up beside Mark and then with arms around their children and each other, they bowed their heads as Eddie thanked God for this baptism in heaven-sent colors. "A peace and joy came over me that I had never felt," says Emmarie. "We had struggled with an ill child, hospital bills, and trying to make ends meet. But now, God had reached down and covered us with a rainbow blanket like a parent tenderly tending his children. I felt His soft breeze caress my face."

When they lifted their heads, the rainbow had disappeared. They climbed back into the car and drove on to the service. After it concluded, they tried to share their experience with others, but were met with a bit of skepticism. Several asked, "How could there be a rainbow that large when it had not rained a drop?"

Says Emmarie, "We can't explain what happened that day. But we know what we experienced. Plus, it was a very real blessing for Debbie, especially. She's in her forties now. While she still has a rare bout of asthma now and then, she has never needed to go to the hospital since the day she danced in the rainbow. I know God blessed Debbie and us in that rainbow."

*J*im Bell and his Irish wife Margaret were newlyweds in the mid-1970s, when Jim was finishing his graduate degree in Ireland. While on spring vacation, they stayed with a fellow American student named Leo, who lived on the west coast of Ireland in a little thatched cottage that had belonged to his grandfather.

Leo had left his Christian roots and become an atheist Marxist. One evening, Jim and Leo got into a friendly debate on the existence of God within the context of Christianity. Leo challenged Jim, saying, "The universe is run by its own natural internal forces, and there is no evidence of a God intervening to go against those laws."

At that point, Margaret spoke up. "Leo, God wants to reveal Himself to you and will intervene to make Himself known," she stated boldly.

In Ireland, rain is as natural and frequent as breathing. The forecast for the following day was a 90-percent chance of rain—all but guaranteeing a rainy day. The group had been hoping for a rare sunny day so that they could go sightseeing among the beautiful lakes and hills.

Margaret prayed, "Oh God, reveal Yourself to Leo. Give us not only a rain-free day tomorrow, but a cloudless, sunny, perfectly blue sky all day to prove Your presence."

Leo let out a great laugh and said there was literally no way it would happen.

The next morning, as they headed out, the sky was cloudless and blue, and the sun shone brightly. The clear day continued as God revealed His beauty through the deep green Irish mountains and lakes.

Leo, a very intelligent and articulate young man, was absolutely dumbfounded. He had no argument against a God who had miraculously revealed Himself.

Later, at dinner, as they all expressed appreciation for a beautiful day and lovely sights, Margaret reminded Leo of her prediction through prayer. He smiled and had nothing to say, but knew his theories were shaken. The Bells still have a picture of themselves in their Irish sweaters on a windswept mountain, reminding them of God's desire to reach everyone with His power.

erri Lynn and Dan Thompson named the second of their three sons Josiah, after a king in Judah who assumed authority at eight years old. Josiah means "The Lord, the One Who heals," or "The Lord, my healer." As all parents do, Terri wondered what unique talents, gifts, and abilities her child would display.

Josiah grew and learned to walk at fourteen months. He followed his brother, Joshua, the sports lover, everywhere he could. Josiah wanted to do everything Joshua did. He tried to run and climb right along with Joshua, but didn't have Joshua's coordination yet.

A few years passed, and one summer Josiah's grandmother taught him to play *Frère Jacques* ("Are You Sleeping?") on the piano. He memorized where his fingers should go, and came home and played the song there as well. Months later, the young boy could still remember and play the song. The very next fall, Terri registered Josiah for a piano class at a local music school.

While Josiah, like many boys, loved baseball and soccer, he also loved classical music and drama. After taking piano lessons for a while, he also wanted to take up the violin. For a couple of years, Josiah saved his birthday and Christmas money and eventually bought his own violin. In the spring of 2003, Terri signed him up for lessons. During the first week, Josiah taught himself the entire song that the instructor had only begun to teach to the class. The instructor was amazed by Josiah's ability to grasp music so quickly.

Then, tragedy struck. Josiah had an accident at a skate park as his parents and brothers looked on. Terri recalls, "I was watching Josiah at the top of a ramp getting ready to roll down. Rather than skate down, he fell straight down, landing hard on his right hand. We all immediately jumped in the car and went straight to the nearest emergency room."

The emergency room doctor couldn't take care of the kind of break Josiah had experienced. The family had to wait eight hours for the on-call specialist. During that

Christian Miracles

wait, Terri and Dan noticed that Josiah couldn't move his two smaller fingers. When the surgeon finally arrived, Terri pointed out the problem.

"Oh my, we better hurry," he said when he looked at Josiah's wrist. The surgeon and nurses took Josiah into a room away from his parents to care for his injuries. Finally the doctor came out to explain Josiah's condition.

"I couldn't set the bone because one portion of it is jammed up under the other," he explained. "I need to do surgery to pry it out."

"What could we say?" says Terri. "Without a choice, my husband and I nodded and then prayed. For the next hours we walked and prayed and cried and prayed some more."

Around four in the morning, they were able to finally take Josiah home. That spring and summer, Josiah went through four different casts. He missed out on baseball and gave up violin completely because holding the bow was impossible. His parents watched his two little fingers every day hoping to see movement, but there was not even any feeling in them.

Josiah learned to play all of his songs on the piano with only his left hand. At his recital he played his solo and his part in the ensemble with just his left hand. His teacher encouraged him, saying this time would make him a better player because he was learning to use that hand so well.

When the cast was removed, the surgeon explained that Josiah displayed typical nerve damage in some of his fingers. He recommended a neurosurgeon, and told them it would take a few weeks before they would be able to get an appointment.

Says Terri, "We had no insurance, and the debt of the first surgery weighed heavily on us. Who would have believed that one broken wrist without an overnight stay in the hospital would add up to $11,000? We had no idea how we'd pay for it. But our greatest concern had nothing to do with money. We wanted Josiah to have full use of his hand."

Terri and her family prayed even more. They called relatives to enlist their prayers and the prayers of their churches. They asked everyone they knew to pray for Josiah.

Terri made the appointment with the neurosurgeon. Later that day, as she was preparing dinner, Terri could hear Josiah playing the piano. "It sounded so full," says Terri. "I tried to hear how many notes were being played at once. Curious how Josiah was doing this, I tiptoed up the stairs to watch him play and suddenly realized he was using both hands and all of his fingers!"

"Josiah," she said, "Are you playing with all your fingers?"

"Yeah," Josiah said and nodded as if it wasn't a big deal.

Tears filled Terri's eyes. That evening she had Dan watch their ten-year-old play.

"We knew a miracle had taken place. In less than a week after the doctor advised us to see the neurosurgeon, Josiah had regained full use of his hand and fingers," says Terri.

Terri called the doctor, explained what happened, and asked if they needed to keep the appointment with the neurosurgeon. The doctor told her to bring Josiah in so he could examine his hands. They saw the doctor that week. After carefully examining Josiah's wrist and fingers, the doctor smiled at Terri and said, "It looks like your prayers are working. Josiah's fingers are functioning normally and he doesn't need any more surgery."

That was not the end of the miracles for the family. Some weeks later Terri and her husband were awarded a grant that covered the hospital bill. The doctors involved agreed to reduce their bills, and then Josiah's grandfather paid them off.

Josiah was able to begin violin lessons again. He continues to excel in piano and violin. Josiah knows from experience that the Lord is truly his Healer.

On a hot humid day in July, Rachel Wallace-Oberle and her husband went to visit his grandmother who lived in a nursing home across town. On the way, they stopped at a convenience store to get a cold drink for their five-year-old son, Thomas. Thomas pulled a bottle from the old-fashioned cooler, they paid, and jumped back in the car.

They realized too late they'd forgotten to open the bottle. Thomas asked pleadingly for Rachel to open his pop. "Oh, Thomas, I can't. We need a can opener." His face fell.

It was a sweltering day and he was thirsty. But even the gift store and ice cream shop were locked, and the nurses' station was deserted. Thomas looked up at his mother woefully. "What should I do, Mommy?"

"Let's say a little prayer." Rachel, her husband, and Thomas bowed their heads as the boy prayed simply, "Please open my pop, God. Amen."

"Hey, little boy," someone suddenly called. "Do you need a can opener?"

They turned to see approaching them an elderly woman in a wheelchair with a gargantuan purse on her lap. A pink cardigan was buttoned up to her chin and yellow slacks covered her spindly legs.

"Bring that pop over here," she instructed, pulling a can opener out of her purse and brandishing it in the air. A length of what appeared to be blue laundry line connected it to the depths from which it had mysteriously emerged.

"You have a can opener in your purse?" Rachel asked, astounded.

"Of course I do," she said matter-of-factly. "Why wouldn't I? You never know when you might need it."

She opened Thomas's pop bottle and handed it back to him. "There you go, young man," she announced. Thomas was speechless with amazement; he couldn't take his eyes off the extraordinary woman who appeared before him. Rachel nudged him to say thank you.

On the way home, Thomas asked, "Why did that little old lady have a can opener in her purse?"

"Because God cares about you so much that even your smallest concern matters to Him," Rachel explained.

*F*or Merlin Gonzales of Indianapolis, Indiana, it had been a busy February day. After dinner, he retired to his bedroom to relax and study. He closed the door, lit a scented jar candle on the nightstand by the bed, and began his theology school studies on the Pauline literature. Annie, his wife, was watching television in the living room. After about an hour of reading, Merlin fell soundly asleep. It was around 9:00 P.M.

Two hours later, Annie turned off the television and began getting ready for bed. She was brushing her teeth in the bathroom when Merlin's cell phone rang. Annie hurried to try to answer it so that it wouldn't wake Merlin up, but he was already reaching for it. The caller hung up before Merlin could answer. He looked up and saw a frightened Annie standing in front of him and staring past him.

"Oh, my!" she exclaimed and pointed to the candle by the bed. Its flame was five inches above the near-empty, and very hot, jar. A scarf was draped over a nearby lamp, precariously close to the flame. Now wide awake, Merlin jumped up and quickly extinguished the candle. It had gotten so hot, it left a burn mark on the night stand.

Relieved, Annie and Merlin both expressed amazement that his cell phone had rung, so late at night, just moments before their bedroom would have caught fire. Curious, Merlin dialed back the person who called. A young lady answered. She said she was trying to respond to a job advertised in the paper, and had dialed a wrong number. How odd, both Annie and Merlin thought, that a person would be calling at such a late hour about a job ad.

"But thanks to the wrong number," says Merlin, "we avoided what could have been a serious disaster. There is no doubt that the jar would have caused a fire in the bedroom. Annie and I both knew right away that it was the Lord who intervened and saved us with a wrong number. We prayed together and praised God for His working in our lives."

The next day Merlin called the young lady back again and shared how the Lord used her to save Merlin and

Annie. He explained all that had happened and thanked her for saving their lives. Annie and Merlin saved the burned jar candle as a reminder of how the Lord is always looking over them.

*C*arol Perdue's dad, Walter Clark, grew up during the Depression with his sisters. The family moved around a bit, living mostly in rural areas. Farming, working in a sawmill, and serving in World War II instilled in Walter a strong work ethic.

After the war, Walter went home to New Castle, Indiana, and started working as the head grower of a local greenhouse. Of her father, Carol says, "He was a very serious man most of the time but loved to pull little pranks that kept me and my little brother, Stephen, on our toes. He worked days at the greenhouse, and was on call all the time. Still, he always found time for his family, and often helped his mom and dad on their small farm just outside of town."

In the mid-1960s, Walter started experiencing stomach problems. The doctor diagnosed ulcers.

"Dad was a man of tremendous faith," says Carol. "When he learned that he had ulcers, he requested prayer at church and then believed for total healing."

Eventually, when he started feeling better, Walter went back to the doctor. The ulcer was gone.

"While dad was a hard worker," says Carol, "he was also very quiet and internalized everything. His mother suffered a series of strokes and died about ten years later. Her death was the most heartbreaking thing he'd ever experienced. I saw my strong daddy break at her memorial service. I'd never seen him so broken in my entire life."

Soon after the funeral, Walter developed ulcers again.

"I took him to the hospital to be examined. Afterwards, Dr. Strong showed us a picture of the hole in my dad's stomach. Dr. Strong said Dad needed to work less and get his stress levels down or he would be in serious condition."

Walter didn't say much. At church, the congregation prayed for him again. His symptoms eased at first, but then the pattern of recurrence continued. He stopped mentioning the pain.

"This went on for some time," says Carol. "We weren't sure what was happening. Mom and I and others were praying desperately for Dad's ulcers to clear up. Then, one

Sunday at church during the testimony time, Dad stood and shared how he had secretly gone back to the doctor for another test. He was healed—without medicine or surgery! And from that day until his death more than twenty years later, he never suffered from ulcers again."

*W*hen she was studying at Fuller Theological Seminary, Sybil Clark took a unique class called "Signs and Wonders for Church Growth." The class met every Monday for three hours of lecture. Afterward, for anyone who wanted to stay, there were practical applications of the power of prayer. The instructor and some trained members of his congregation would pray with people for healing. The class of 250 people was the largest the seminary had ever had up until that point.

While she was enrolled in the class, Sybil developed an abscessed tooth. "My tooth swelled with infection and pain and I rushed in to see my dentist," she explains. "He took an X ray, and it was clear that the lining around the tooth was broken. It had indeed abscessed. He told me I needed a root canal. When you are a poor seminary student, you don't have $450 sitting around to pay a dentist. The doctor gave me antibiotics and scheduled me for the root canal the next week."

A few days after the dentist appointment, Sybil attended her Monday night class. "Throughout the lecture I had an interesting feeling in my body. I felt tingly all over, and I was trembling. I knew from what was taught in class this was one of the evidences of the presence of the Holy Spirit resting with someone."

"At the conclusion of his teaching, the instructor said he would be doing things a little differently that evening. He told us there were people present upon whom the Holy Spirit had been resting throughout the lecture, and he asked them to come forward.

"Yippee!" thought Sybil, "I'll get my abscessed tooth healed." She got up immediately and went to the front of the class. About forty other people also went forward.

"When my turn came," says Sybil, "The pastor said something was wrong with my hips. I told him that I didn't have any trouble with my hips but that I had an abscessed tooth that needed healing. He said he'd pray for the tooth but there was definitely a problem with my hips and he'd pray for that too. I didn't see the sense for this because I wasn't aware of a problem."

While the pastor was praying, Sybil felt her tooth tingling. The sensation spread throughout the right side of her face. Her tooth felt great.

A few days later she went back to her dentist. Before he started the root canal, Sybil explained what happened. At Sybil's urging, her skeptical dentist took another X ray. He was reluctant to say what the X ray showed. He told Sybil, "You take a different angle, you get a different picture." She didn't get the root canal.

Sybil also saw her regular doctor to ask about her hip. He had her stand while he put his thumbs on the top of each side of her hips. "Yes," he said, "your left leg is about one-half inch shorter than the right leg."

"Oh, I've known that since I was a teenager," said Sybil. "I always had to hem my slacks shorter on the left." An X ray confirmed the difference. The doctor explained that having a shorter leg would throw Sybil's back out of alignment and curve her spine slightly, causing back pain.

Sybil remembered that she had experienced severe back pain during her pregnancy, and that the pain continued after she had given birth. Her doctor told her that there was no cure for something like this and gave her a number of daily exercises to ease the pain.

"The next Monday in class," says Sybil, "I talked to a fellow classmate. He was a medical doctor. He told me that as soon as he looked at me, the week before, he could see that my hips were not even. He went on to describe what that does to the back. He even drew me a little picture to show me that the uneven hips caused the slight curvature and even indicated the spot on the back where the pain would be. Sure enough, that's where I felt the pain."

Despite additional prayer with the instructor and others in the class, nothing happened to Sybil's leg. However, Sybil was part of another prayer group that had been meeting to pray for an hour each week for a woman in another country. During one of these prayer sessions, Sybil sensed something happening in her leg.

"I noticed that there was a tingly feeling beginning in my left leg. The tingling went up and down my left leg. Then, the tingling started across my pelvis bone, back and forth. Both my left leg and my pelvis were tingling. I opened my eyes and told the group that the Holy Spirit was touching my leg and asked if they could come and lay hands on me and pray for the healing right then. I stood up and they all stood around me with their hands on my shoulders. As they began to pray for me I felt my left leg extend. Then, it was over, just like that. I put my thumbs on my hips. They were even. I asked others in the group if they could push their thumbs down on my hips and see if they could tell if they were even. Everyone said that they were. I was ecstatic!"

About six years later, while she was having other dental work done, Sybil asked her new dentist to look at the lining around the formerly abscessed tooth and tell her if there was any sign it had ever abscessed. Once a tooth abscesses, the lining around the tooth breaks, and this shows up as a bright white spot on an X ray. Her new dentist told her that none of the teeth on the upper right side showed any evidence that they had ever abscessed. Her teeth were all healthy.

Sybil went through two more pregnancies with no back pain.

*B*etty King's daughter had been raised in a Christian home. After getting married and starting a family, she rededicated her life to the Lord. A busy housewife and mother of two little boys, she found herself with little time and a feeling of being an inadequate Christian witness. She began to pray the Lord would open up opportunities for her to tell others of her faith and love for Him.

On an errand one day at the Bible Book Store, she spotted a key chain bearing the phrase, "Praise The Lord." Did she dare spend $5 on something she really didn't need? It would be a subtle way to witness, and it wouldn't be offensive to anyone while still getting her point across.

Even total strangers would be aware of her faith, without her having to say a single word. Perhaps this was the start on her way to being the kind of witness she wanted to be.

Her husband drove her car to his office a few nights later. It was a bitter cold night, so before heading back home, he decided to start the car and let it warm a bit. He went back into the office for only a few moments. When he came back outside, the car was gone.

That evening Betty's daughter and her husband discussed the disappearance of their car. They knew that if it were found at all, it most likely would have been stripped or damaged. Still, that night they prayed, asking God to return their car to them unharmed.

The next morning they received an early phone call. Someone across town had found the car parked in their driveway with the doors open, keys still in it, engine running. There was not a scratch on the car. The only thing missing was the "Praise The Lord" key chain. Perhaps for this thief, stealing the key chain rather than the car was a reminder never to steal again.

Says Betty King, "We never know how or in what subtle way our lives may reach out to others. God can take the simplest occurrences and magnify their effect. Prayers, too, are far reaching; they can have consequences of great magnitude. We should never forget also, that in faith, mountains have moved."

onica Cane had been in a deep sleep on a warm July night in 1997 when she awoke from a peculiar dream. In her dream, she had smelled a distinct foul odor in the air. The smell was so intense that it startled her awake. At first, she wasn't even sure whether the smell had been real or if it was just in her dream.

"An uneasiness crept over me," she says. "I crawled out from beneath the covers and decided to check on the children. I peeked into their room and they looked like perfect little lambs tucked under their covers."

Monica went through every room in the quiet, dark house. Finding nothing out of the ordinary, she headed back to bed. Yet the sense of uneasiness intensified and the memory of the foul smell flooded her senses. She went through the house again.

"I walked into the living room, the center of our little house, and scanned in every direction. I sniffed the air repeatedly trying to detect something. There was nothing unusual in the air."

Still, she was increasingly troubled in her spirit, and the sense of the odor would not leave her. Quietly, in the middle of her sleeping home, Monica prayed, "What is it God? Show me the smell." The answer came swiftly.

"I felt overwhelmingly drawn back to the kids' room. When I walked in, they looked just as peaceful as they had before. My four-year-old daughter, Kalaya, was snuggled up in a ball under her covers. My nine-year-old daughter, Krystal, was clinging to her favorite blue teddy bear. I didn't see or smell anything alarming but felt an almost magnetic pull toward Krystal and her blue bear."

Monica removed the teddy bear from her daughter's hands. She was shocked to discover that it was actually smoldering on the inside. The bear had been propped against a nightlight and the heat from the light caused the bear's fabric to smolder.

The teddy bear surely would have eventually burst into flames in the hands of the little girl.

"God used my dream to warn me of the potential danger. And when I prayed for guidance as to the danger, He showed me exactly where it was," says Monica. "We no longer use the same type of nightlights, and we no longer have the blue teddy bear. But we have the testimony of God's miracle keeping our family safe in the midst of unseen danger."

*K*aren John couldn't sleep. One o'clock in the morning soon became two and then three and four and five, until the birds ushered in a February Sunday sunrise. She turned to her husband, nudging him awake, "It's time to get up for church."

As he stirred, Karen began recounting to him the events of her night.

"You won't believe my morning prayer-vigil. I have been praying for the three sons of Dorothy Davis," she said. "In fact, I woke up at one praying for them and pleading with God for their well-being. I sense the need to keep praying, so I did the rest of the night."

"Who's Dorothy Davis?" her husband asked, still struggling to get his bearings.

"She's the mom of Larry Davis. You know, from church. She has two other sons who have moved down South: Steve, Larry's twin brother, and Chris, their younger brother," Karen answered.

"Now, why were you praying for them?"

"I really don't know. It's baffling. All I can tell you is that I was praying for their welfare."

After breakfast they hurried off to Sunday school and church. Typically, the adult class began the morning with coffee and discussion. They offered prayers of blessing and of concern before beginning the day's Bible lesson.

"I have a unique prayer concern this morning," Larry Davis explained as he arrived just after Karen and her husband. "My mother has just suffered a stroke and is asking that others pray for me and my two brothers, Steve and Chris. The part of her brain that gives her the ability to pray has been damaged by the stroke."

Immediately, Karen and her husband turned to each other as tears welled up in their eyes while the rest of the class looked on with concern.

"I was awakened by the Spirit of the Lord early this morning for this very purpose," Karen explained. "My husband can tell you . . . I have already begun to answer your mother's request."

There was no way that Karen could have possibly known that Dorothy Davis needed her prayers that morning. Even so, the Lord made sure to answer what was on her heart. Not long after Dorothy's request for prayer, Dorothy discovered that she had cancer. When she lay dying, she still had the strength to reassure her loved ones that all was well. "I have had a really good life," she said, "I don't want you to feel sorrowful for me. I am ready to be with God."

The day after Resurrection Sunday in 1997, Maria Gonzales was leaving when she discovered that her van was no longer in the parking lot. It had been stolen. This was a major problem for Maria—she only had liability insurance on the van, and she needed it to get to and from work.

Maria's office was only a couple of blocks away from her church. "Every day at lunchtime," she says, "I would go and get alone with God and claim the promises of Psalms 91. I kept reminding Him that His word promised that He would take care of everything that was under my tent, and as old as it was, that van was under my tent."

Every time Maria shared her situation with someone, it seemed everyone fully expected the worst. Says Maria, "Everyone kept telling me that the van, if it was found at all, would be found stripped or burnt up or dumped in a river somewhere. I believed otherwise and kept taking my petition to the Lord every day."

A week went by with no news about the van. Maria trusted God but says she thought, "Maybe it is not His will for me to get my car back."

She and her husband attended a prayer meeting that Friday evening. They had been there a few times before. "For some reason," says Maria, "my husband chose to take an unusual route through some of the roughest parts of town. And lo and behold, as we turned onto one street, right up ahead of us was our van! Our mouths dropped. We quickly went to the nearest payphone to call the police."

A short time later, the police arrived and recovered the van. While writing out the report, one officer commented, "I don't know what we're doing here. Fridays are our busiest nights, and here we are recovering a vehicle that's not considered a priority." Maria told him that she had been praying and that it was God who had brought them there.

"The van was just the way it was when it was stolen," declares Maria. "It was not burned or stripped like people had said. God is awesome!"

—*by Maria Gonzales as told to Monica Cane*

*T*he winter of 1986 had been a long and hard one. Linda and Steve Knight felt their circumstances matched the landscape.

"My husband had been laid off for five months," recalls Linda. "Money was scarce, our cupboards were nearly bare, and my faith was dwindling. Even though my husband was in the skilled trades, a slump in the auto industry had caused massive layoffs. Our future looked bleak."

Then, some friends called. They lived a good distance away and had decided to drive down for a visit. "Much as I loved them and wanted to see them, I dreaded not being able to offer them much more than a cup of coffee," says Linda.

Linda turned to God in prayer. She sat on her couch in the living room and opened her Bible to John 16:23: "I tell you the truth, my Father will give you whatever you ask in my name" (NIV).

Blinking back tears, Linda prayed, "Father, this may seem kind of silly to You, but what I'd really like to be able to serve our company today is some treats. Soda and chips and cookies and lots and lots of goodies, that's what I'd like. Oh, and chicken and potatoes and some vegetables would be nice too. And, the icing on the cake would be a job for my husband. Thank You, Father."

Just having prayed, her spirit seemed somehow lighter. Twenty minutes later there was a knock at the back door.

"There stood my husband's parents," says Linda, "They carried in six bags full of groceries!"

"I know it's been really hard on you kids lately," her mother-in-law said. "I know you need all kinds of stuff but sometimes what we really need is a treat. So, we decided to treat you today."

Looking through the bags, Linda and her husband were astonished. They now had soda, chips, cookies, donuts, and lots of other assorted goodies. Plus a huge bucket of take-out chicken, coleslaw, mixed vegetables, and macaroni salad. There was even a chocolate cake.

"My in-laws knew nothing about our having friends on the way to visit us that day," says Linda, "but God did. He knew before they even called, and He'd already prepared the hearts of my in-laws to help meet those needs even before I prayed!"

Linda and her husband had a wonderful visit with their friends. Two weeks later, her husband was back working full time.

"When God says He'll meet our needs," proclaims Linda, "He means it!"

n Thursday, October 16, 2003, Deno Barroga received a phone call from his sister, Deanna, at the hospital where he worked, in Dallas, Texas.

"My sister sounded hysterical and said that my mom was at the hospital dying," says Deno. "My heart sank, and I asked my sister to tell me what happened. My sister, who is a nurse, mentioned an aortic dissection and that my mom had to be taken to the emergency room. Despite believing Matthew 19:26, which says 'With man this is impossible, but with God all things are possible,' as a physician I knew that aortic dissections are often fatal. I called my twin brother, Desi, who is also a physician, in

New Jersey. We discussed making travel plans to fly back home to Hawaii."

Later that night, Deno packed for the trip. "As I finished my preparations, I heard my mom's voice speak to me saying, 'Boy, don't forget the letter.' It took a minute, but then I recalled the letter my mom wrote to me after she visited me in Dallas last year. I found the letter and put it in my suitcase," says Deno.

The next morning, Deno flew to Hawaii. When he arrived at the hospital, he found friends and family members gathered in a waiting area. Then he went in to visit his mother. "I saw her there," recounts Deno, "lying in the hospital bed. Lines and tubes all around her. The sound of the breathing machine and occasional alarms and beeps painted a poor prognosis in my mind."

Later, back in the waiting area, Deno's sister shared with him what had happened. Around 2:00 A.M., while she was working in a local grocery store in Kapolei, Hawaii, their mother had experienced the initial pain of the aortic dissection. An ambulance rushed her to the hospital. The emergency room personnel had to perform CPR on her five times. After being transported to a larger hospital, she underwent emergency surgery and was then placed in the critical care unit.

There, she again had several episodes of dangerous and life-threatening irregular heartbeats that required external heart-regulating devices to be placed over her chest. She also required respiratory support from a large bedside ventilation machine.

"Things did not look good," says Deno. "In fact, things looked awful." His mother's blood pressure became difficult to manage. She suffered partial kidney failure and infections. While the stress took its toll on the family, they kept praying for a miracle.

One day, while he sat in the waiting room, Deno took out his prayer journal, which contained a collection of favorite Scriptures he had compiled. "I had placed the letter that my mom wrote to me in the front cover," says Deno. "My sister noticed it and asked if she could read it to the entire family."

Hi, Son Deno, thank you so much for a lovely visit. Mom and Dad really enjoyed every precious moment with you. Never be sad son, life is too short. Change your tears upside down into a 'happy face.' Hee hee hee. Always remember you are out of sight but not out of mind. We are only a phone call away. You are also just a heartbeat away from Mom and Dad. Yesterday is gone with memories and the present we live each day with Jesus, and if this was our last day on earth, be happy. The future is yet to be when we will see each other in twelve months. Time goes by so fast. P.S. Roses are red, violets are blue, I thank God for giving me a son like you. I love you Deno. Hee hee hee. With all our love, Mom and Dad.

After reading the letter, Deno's sister looked up surprised. "Deno, did you know Mom wrote this letter on October 16, 2002, exactly twelve months to the day before her dissection?"

In disbelief, Deno looked at the date on the letter. He could scarcely believe his eyes. Still, days passed with no improvement in his mother's condition. Since she had been admitted to the hospital, she had suffered a stroke, a heart attack, kidney failure, lung failure, pneumonia, a blood infection, and possible brain damage due to a lack of oxygen.

Finally, two of the critical care physicians, the neurologist, the cardiologist, and the cardiothoracic surgeon gave grim outlooks. They each separately recommended considering removal of all life support. "My dad took the news especially hard," says Deno. "The doctors suggested that we wait over the weekend to see if my mom would make any progress and then, if no progress could be seen, discontinuing life support. Quietly, I prepared myself for the inevitable."

As he was praying, Deno heard a voice say, "Your mom will be with you by next week, Wednesday."

"I thought I was crazy," says Deno. "Delusional and hearing things. After all, I had not had much sleep since arriving in Hawaii. Yet, something told me to share this news with others. So I told my dad, my brother, my sisters, and friends about the voice and what it told me."

The days passed, and Wednesday arrived. Deno's mother began to be able to move her arms and legs, and she quietly asked for water. She was able to nod her head yes or shake it no in response to questions.

"Over the next month, she made miraculous strides," says Deno. "Nurses from the other floors came by saying they just wanted to see the miracle lady. The doctors had no explanation in Mom's sudden turnaround."

Later, Deno's brother, Desi, asked his mother if she knew she had died.

"Yes," she replied.

"Where did you go? What did you see?"

"I went through a tunnel and bright light surrounded me," said his mother. "I saw two angels in white gowns telling me to come inside. I did not feel any stress, only beauty, joy, and peace."

More than two years later, Deno's mom and dad enjoy going to movies together. His mother no longer requires hemodialysis for her kidneys. Her blood pressure is well controlled, and she has no residual brain damage. She is truly a miracle woman.

"Mom, Mom, oh! Thank God, we're still alive. I had to hear your voice to be sure," said Patricia Ruth Johnson's daughter, Nancy.

"What happened?" Patricia asked, trying to stay calm.

"There's been a horrible accident," said Nancy.

"Nancy, are you and Tim all right?"

"Yes, but I don't know how. It's got to be a miracle."

Nancy went on to explain. They had been traveling on the interstate near Bakersfield, California, when suddenly they were enveloped in a dust storm. With zero visibility, and without warning, they were suddenly seconds away from ramming into a tangle of cars that had smashed into a jack-knifed truck spread across the highway. There was no place to go.

"Time seemed to go into slow motion," said Nancy. "Tim pulled into a small opening that almost looked like a parking space just big enough for our little car."

The couple braced themselves for speeding cars coming from the rear, but all of them veered to the side of the pocket. Nancy and Tim were completely untouched.

The air cleared long enough for them to see they had a chance to pull beyond the shoulder of the highway. As soon as they were safe, the wind once again swirled fiercely around them. They sat stunned, listening as one car after another plowed into the wreckage. Ultimately, there were more than 100 vehicles involved.

"Oh Mom! It was awful. With the sound of every crash we knew people were being hurt or killed," Nancy said.

Nancy and Tim arrived home safely that Saturday night. "We were all very grateful for their miraculous protection," says Patricia. "Before I fell asleep that night, visions of what had happened to Nancy and Tim ran through my mind, and I knew God had sent angels to protect them."

The next Tuesday morning, Patricia went to her women's Bible study. "I could hardly wait to share my story with my friends. As I began, three women who were new to our group came in quietly and took a seat. When I finished sharing, everyone rejoiced with me for God's intervention. Then one of the new women, who introduced herself as Myrene, began to tell her amazing story."

"On Saturday evening," explained Myrene, "my husband and I were sitting at home when I felt an urgent impression to begin to pray. I asked my husband, Hank, to join me. As we prayed together I began to see a picture in my mind of a truck jack-knifed across a highway. We continued to pray until we felt released." She ended her prayer time that evening saying, "Lord, many times we have prayed like this, and have never known who it was we've prayed for. Would You allow me to know this time?"

He did, and now she knew.

*G*eorgia Ethel McDaniel, the third child of six, was born on May 12, 1905. She was strong willed, creative, spirited, and not afraid to speak her mind. She was Donna Caudill's grandmother.

Donna enjoyed listening to her grandmother talk about her heritage. "She gave me a glimpse into the times past of this precious lady. They were pictures that lived in her memories. I heard about riding to church in a horse-drawn wagon, playing 'Drop the Handkerchief' in the school-yard, and learning to sew on a treadle sewing machine. I held on to every word and tried to imagine I was there with her," recalls Donna.

About a year before Georgia died, she told Donna a true story about Donna's great-grandmother, Nellie.

Nellie McDaniel had fallen ill with a heart disorder. Her doctor said she'd have to undergo heart surgery unless she showed significant improvement within a few weeks.

With this diagnosis, Nellie was bedridden, and her feet never touched the floor for the next nine weeks. When it was time to make her bed, she was picked up and carried to the chair that sat beside the bed. Her children, Ethel, Alma, and Nettie, played games on the floor beside her bed. They were ten, seven, and three. In spite of their youth, they took care of their mother while their dad, Israel, worked in the fields of their large farm.

"Propped pillows" was Nellie's only repeated request. Ethel made sure the pillowcases were washed and ironed. To pass the time, Nellie would read her Bible, especially the many accounts of healing. She began to realize she too could be healed if she believed.

One afternoon, while the girls were playing by her bed, Nellie sat straight up. The countenance of her face suddenly changed. She instructed, "Nettie, bring Mammy her dress! She's healed."

Three-year-old Nettie ran to the chair and scooted it across the floor so that she could reach the dress, which hung on a nail in the wall.

That evening, as Israel and his brother were returning home, they saw with astonished eyes that Nellie was standing at the stove, cooking supper.

A few days later, Nellie and the whole family headed into town for a scheduled doctor's appointment. Israel went into the doctor's office first, and the doctor asked, "How is Nellie?"

"She's out in the waiting area. Would you like to talk to her?" replied Israel.

He followed Israel into the waiting area, expecting to see an ill, weak, and frail patient in need of heart surgery. He was totally amazed when he found a beaming mother sitting with her children.

Nellie lived for fifty-three more years with no further heart problems. She died at the age of eighty-six, having been living proof that it only takes simple faith to see big miracles.

arsha Joy Baker's husband, Ron, had been an insulin-dependent diabetic for nearly ten years. Ron worked in a factory all day, standing on a rubber mat to relieve the discomfort of his feet.

June of 2001 was unusually hot, and the heat added to the pain Ron suffered from the diabetic neuropathy (nerve damage) in his feet. Says Marsha, "He has a very high tolerance of pain. I learned that after he'd gone through back surgery. He was in church only two days later, lying on the front pew claiming that it was only a little pain."

When Ron came home from work early one day that June and told Marsha that the factory nurse said he was to take off from work for the summer, Marsha knew things were getting bad. By the fall, the family doctor insisted that he go on permanent disability and not push himself to work any longer.

Ron agreed and filled out the paperwork for disability and filed it as early as possible. And then they waited. Ron completed additional paperwork, and they waited some more. While they waited, money grew tighter and tighter. They had been receiving temporary disability checks, but these had run out.

Says Marsha, "I asked for prayer for our situation at church the Sunday after we'd received the last check for temporary disability. Without hesitating, our pastor told the congregation, 'We need to help this dear couple,' and then said to our deacons, 'I think we need to give them $500.'"

Ron had not been feeling well enough to go to church. When she got home from church, Marsha was in tears as she showed him the $500 check plus an additional $100 in cash.

"We still waited several weeks before the paperwork was finalized, but I believe God's perfect timing allowed that to happen so that He could be glorified. In those very long weeks while we waited for the final approval, we received so many blessings!" says Marsha.

In addition to the money from their church, more miracles followed. Two friends sent sizeable checks. Marsha won a set of lovely snowman dishes from a nationally known cooking magazine. She also won an overstuffed reindeer from their local drugstore for Christmas. Marsha's beautician gave her a free haircut, just because she wanted to be in on the blessings the couple was receiving. Once, when she was grocery shopping, Marsha used manufacturers' coupons and in-store coupons and saved more money than she had spent.

Declares Marsha, "There wasn't an ounce of doubt in our minds, that each and every one of those folks were used to bless us and they received blessings as well. One of my favorite verses is Nahum 1:7: 'The LORD is good, a refuge in times of trouble. He cares for those who trust in him' (NIV). What a special blessing it is to know He cares about all the details in our lives!"

arie Thomas and Dave worked together in the manufacturing area of a large computer company. They were only two of about fifty board testers who worked at twenty-five test benches. At first, they barely spoke except about work. But after a year and a half, they became close friends.

Dave was a slim twenty-two-year-old, with Italian good looks and a gentle heart. He had a shock of thick, neatly trimmed dark hair. "His large, steady brown eyes said you could trust him with your life," says Marie. "But he also had a shy side that spoke of secret fears and insecurities."

Dave's mother had left his family when he was very young, and his father never emotionally recovered. Without much parental nurture, he had to become an adult at about six years old. As they got to know each other, Marie realized Dave was searching for God. For months, no matter what they talked about, the subject came up frequently.

To take the job at the computer company, Dave had left his childhood home in a large city to move across the state and get his first apartment in a rural town where he knew no one. He was an only child, so he left behind only his father and a large, impersonal denominational church full of crowds and ceremony and ritual—a church that had told him it was "God's will" that he grow up without a mother. The idea of finding God in all that manmade pomp was next to impossible.

"I wasn't a Sunday churchgoer," says Marie. "I attended an evening Bible study and had a small close circle of Christian friends, some of whom also worked with us. Dave observed our family-like relationships and obviously wanted to be part of it, but we met on Friday nights when he worked his second job."

Marie suggested he attend a similar meeting that took place Tuesday nights. "Tomorrow's Tuesday!" Dave said excitedly, "How do I get there?" All that day and the next, he was just as excited as if he were going to a ball game. When they left work that afternoon, Dave said to Marie, "Maybe I'll find God tonight like you have."

"On Wednesday, Dave was in when I got there," says Marie. "I had never seen him smile the way he was smiling then, like he had a secret. His eyes were sharp and they twinkled with life as if he was bursting to say something. I set up my test bed and went to get coffee."

When Marie returned, Dave blurted out, "I did it. I prayed with them last night," he said. "And now I know Jesus as my Savior too. It was so easy. They never told me about that in my church. It scares me that I could have gone my whole life and never known what I learned last night.

"I never got to bed," Dave continued. "Once I got home, I just had to read the Bible they gave me. It's almost identical to one I used to have, but I could never understand my old one. God opened it up to me last night. I couldn't stop. I read until four in the morning before I realized it. I knew if I tried to sleep then, I'd never wake up in time for work, so I just took a shower and came in. I've been in since just before five this morning."

From that day on, Dave was like a different person. His face practically shone. He smiled all the time, to himself or at others. And for a once-shy, introverted man, he suddenly had people all around him wanting to get some of whatever he had. He lived to be in worship meetings with other believers. He often spent his lunch hour in his car, reading the Bible.

When Dave's new church asked him to help with visitations, he was thrilled. He went out that weekend. The following Monday, he shared the experience with Marie.

The pastor had driven Dave and four others to a neighborhood where they set off on foot in twos. After visiting several streets, Dave and his partner thought they might be late returning to the car if they didn't split up to cover the last two short dead-end streets. His partner took one street, and Dave took the other.

Dave walked alone up to the first house and knocked, but no one was home. He heard a dog barking somewhere nearby and was a little nervous. He was petrified of dogs. But it stopped and he headed toward the last house on the street with a beautiful lawn and a low picket fence in front. He entered by a gate and walked up to knock on the front door when he heard horrible barking and growling coming from around the side of the house.

Panicked, Dave backed through the gate again and froze in the middle of the street as a huge, growling German shepherd appeared around the side of the house, and sailed over the foot-high fence, launching itself right at him. He couldn't move and all he could manage to say was "Jesus, help me."

The dog landed on the dirt road right in front of Dave, ready to spring, when suddenly it fell to a crouch right at his feet and looked up in fear—not at Dave, but at something right above his head. The huge dog was frozen, ears flat, cowering. Then it started backing away, its fearful eyes locked on something just above Dave's head.

"Seeing the dog's reaction," says Dave, "I was curious but at the same time frightened myself by whatever it was behind me!"

As soon as the dog turned and ran away, Dave turned hesitantly to look behind him. There was nothing, no one behind him or above him. Not a telephone pole. Not a tree. Nothing.

He looked up and down the street, up into the sky, surveyed the yards and alleys on all sides. He was completely alone on a warm, quiet afternoon, yet he could still hear the fleeing dog's frightened yipping in the distance.

"You know," Dave said, "I've never seen an angel, but I think I've felt one. In the middle of that experience, in the middle of the fear, I remember being kind of calm. I felt a peace that I was okay, protected, you know? No matter what." He paused and said, "But I guess the dog saw the angel."

Not too long after that, Dave went off to a Bible school near where he had grown up. Three years later, he was ordained as a minister. He married a girl from his Bible school and has two beautiful children with her—and they own a German shepherd.

*O*n April 2, 1994, Pat DeMello's nineteen-year-old son, Nick, was getting ready to go out with his friends. He mentioned he was tired, and Pat suggested he take a nap before leaving. He assured his mother he was fine, gave her a kiss, and headed out. At 3:45 A.M., the phone rang.

"It was Nick's friend, Jason," recalls Pat. "He told me that Nick had gotten very sleepy and pulled off to the side of the road to rest. A man who had been drinking heavily fell asleep at the wheel and hit Nick's car on the driver's side, going fifty-five miles an hour, sending Nick's car into a spin."

Pat woke up her oldest son, James, explained what happened, and they both began to pray. "Lord, please let Nick be all right," they tearfully plead.

"James continued to pray," explains Pat, "as I began to make phone calls to try and find out where they had taken Nick. He had been airlifted, and his injuries were extensive."

Pat and James arrived at the hospital about thirty minutes later. A doctor explained to Pat that Nick had just had a seizure, but not to worry, they would take good care of him. "I just cried and prayed, asking God to please let Nick be all right," says Pat. About an hour later, a nurse told Pat she could go in and see Nick. "My son, my baby, was black and blue, and his face was swollen almost beyond recognition. His bloody clothes had been cut off of him and they were lying at his side. I broke down and started to cry as the nurse put her arms around me to comfort me," says Pat.

Later, the doctor detailed Nick's injuries. His left leg was broken; he had a broken shoulder blade, broken wrist, fractured check bones, shattered sinuses, a bruised lung, and lots of internal bleeding. Swelling of his brain had caused the seizure, so doctors had inserted a shunt to relieve the pressure until the swelling went down. There would be no way of knowing whether he had any brain damage until he woke up.

"When I got home later," says Pat, "I called my mother and told her what happened. She started calling everyone in the family to report the news and ask everyone to pray for Nick. Before I knew it, I had family and friends at my house gathering together to pray for Nick's complete recovery. Over the next few days, people began calling from all over, offering comfort for me and prayers for Nick. As the word spread through word of mouth, telephone, and even e-mail, we had people of all faiths and all across the country praying! What a blessing to see God's people coming together in prayer from everywhere."

On Easter Sunday, Nick's aunt, Leslie, went to church and told the congregation what had happened to her nephew and asked them to pray for a complete healing. After the service was over, one of the men from the church told Leslie that he had spent the night in the same jail cell as the man who was driving the car that hit Nick. Explains Pat, "The man from the church had an argument with his wife and the police were called. The law required that if the police were called out, he had to go to jail for the night to ensure nothing more would happen. It never happened before that night or since. I know the Lord placed him there for that purpose."

The man from church reported that as soon as the driver who had hit Pat's son was put into the cell he began crying. He explained what happened and that he didn't know if the young driver of the other car was dead. The man from the church asked the driver if he wanted to pray together for the young man. They got on their knees in the jail cell and began to pray for Nick. God certainly has a way of putting His people where they are needed.

Nick was in an induced coma for four days after the car accident. On the fifth day, he completely woke up. He underwent corrective surgery for his skull and sinuses and was expected to be released a few days later, but the day after the surgery, his condition worsened.

"He was getting more and more lethargic," says Pat. "They gave him one test after another and still could not determine the reason for his condition. I got on my knees and prayed that the Lord would show the doctor what was wrong. I pleaded with Him not to take my son."

Nick went back into surgery. Hours later, the doctor explained to Pat that they had discovered another fracture in Nick's skull. The doctor described it as the kind of fracture that boxers get in the boxing ring when they hit the mat, unconscious, after a knockout. The doctor had never seen a fracture like that anywhere except in his textbook on autopsies, and he said it was a miracle that Nick was still alive. But the young man was in a coma again.

One month after the accident, Nick finally began to come out of the coma. This once thriving youth could not speak or move, and his 6'3" body had dwindled from 150 to 103 pounds. After weeks of high fevers, much therapy, and countless hours of prayer, he began to recover.

"On Sunday, just eighty-six days after the accident," says Pat, "we were able to get Nick out of the hospital on a day pass. Nick walked through the doors of the church in Sunnyvale, and was greeted with a standing ovation. Then, three months after the accident instead of six months as earlier predicted, Nick was released from the hospital and I took him home."

Today, at age thirty, the only physical reminders that Nick bears are the loss of vision in his left eye and the loss of smell. He is currently an accounting business analyst at University of Phoenix in Pleasanton, California, and a living miracle.

—by Pat DeMello as told to Monica Cane

In September of 1980, Sybil Clark was living in an attic suite of a two-story house. A woman with two children lived on the main floor. One of Sybil's high school friends lived on the second floor with another girl. On a weekday morning, at around 6:20 A.M., Sybil heard a large explosion and felt the whole house shake.

"I was just lying in bed, wondering what in the world had happened. Moments later, my friend knocked on my door and told me to come down right away. There was panic in her voice. I went down to see what she sounded distressed about. Black smoke was pouring through the heating vents in their second floor suite. She told me we had to get out of there right away. The house was on fire!"

Sybil ran back up to her room to grab some valuables and make a quick call to the fire department. When she came back down, her friend had already left. Sybil started downstairs to the main floor, but the stairwell was completely black with smoke.

"There was zero visibility," she says, "I covered my nose and mouth with my sweater and climbed down through the smoke. I got to the front door and couldn't get the doorknob unlocked. By this time I was breathing in a lot of smoke. I prayed, silently asking the Lord what to do. Then I remembered there was a fire escape. I headed back upstairs and went down the ladder attached to the outside of the house. The other two women were in the backyard, relieved to see me."

All three were thankful to be out of the house, but then they remembered the woman and her kids on the first floor. Sybil headed for the back door. "I smashed the glass on the door and reached in to unlock it. If it was possible, I was going to try to get them out of there. As soon as I put my hand on the doorknob the Holy Spirit spoke to me so clearly and said, 'They aren't here.' I stopped."

Soon the fire department arrived and doused the fire. In the end, the main floor was completely gutted by the fire. So was the basement. Everything that the woman on the main floor owned was completely destroyed. The second-floor rooms smelled heavily of smoke, but everything was in perfect condition. The attic room was fine as well. The woman had left at 6:00 A.M. to take her kids to day care. And the girls who had been home were miraculously protected.

mily Holland drove from Indiana to Maryland after learning that her father had been admitted to the hospital. On a routine follow-up visit to his diabetes doctor, a black spot on her father's toe caused concern. Tests showed that the blood clots in his right foot caused poor circulation and had cut off oxygen to his toe. He had gangrene, and the doctor was concerned that gangrene would set into the leg. Surgery was scheduled.

Emily's sisters tried to contact her, unaware that she was already on the way to see their father. Everyone was surprised when she walked into the hospital room unannounced. "The Lord called me to be there," says Emily.

About twelve inches of her father's artery in his right leg were obstructed, and the doctor determined he needed to perform a bypass. The surgery was only supposed to take about four hours. Instead, nearly seven hours into the operation, a nurse informed the family that the surgeon was not satisfied with the flow of blood to his foot and was creating another graft in an attempt to improve circulation. If the surgery was unsuccessful, Emily's father would lose his foot.

"Waiting for the surgery to end," says Emily, "I was quietly having my doubts and considered the grim reality that my father might lose his foot or even his leg. I wondered how my mother, who was seventy-two, would be able to cope with such a disability."

After the surgery was completed, the doctor explained to Emily and her family that the veins and capillaries were in worse shape than expected, and that there was a 50-percent chance the leg would have to be amputated.

"Returning to my parents' home late that evening with my exhausted mother," says Emily, "I prayerfully drifted off to sleep. I knew that I must be strong to cope with any adversity that was ahead."

The next evening, the doctor informed the family that the prospects for saving the leg looked no better and that new gangrene appeared to be evident. Emily prayed again during the night. Neither she nor her mother could sleep.

Emily called her sister, Terri, the next morning and asked that she start the prayer chain at her church.

Only three hours after that call, Emily's father called home and said the doctor had been in and thought the foot looked very good. "His foot was now pink," says Emily, "indicating good blood flow, and there was no visible sign of gangrene. I had never before experienced the miracle of prayer in such a way. It was amazing that there could be such a dramatic change in only a few hours.

"The Lord truly healed my father's foot," continues Emily. "His right foot now has life and is youthful in appearance. It is truly a miracle, the great healing power of the Lord."

Annettee Budzban was a single mother with tight finances when a large old oak tree blew over in her backyard.

"The wind was blowing extremely hard. I could hear the trees creaking. A few times, I was awakened by the sound of crashing thunder. Each time I awoke, I prayed for protection over the two bedrooms that were close to the tree," says Annette. "When I got up the next morning, I could see why God had placed it on my heart to pray. That old tree had cracked and broken in two. Half of the tree was lying in my yard, with its debris of broken limbs and shredded bark scattered all over the place, and the other half was strewn on top of my neighbor's garage. As I looked at the remainder of the mighty oak, the mess in my yard, and my neighbor's garage roof, I really wasn't sure what I was going to do other than trust God for an answer."

Annettee called several local services getting quotes on having the tree removed. Getting someone to come out, cut up the tree, and remove all the pieces would cost $500 or more. She did not have the money. "Fortunately," she says, "the neighbors didn't press me about the mess my tree had made on their garage."

After a few days, her friend Jeannie came by to take Annettee out. "Jeannie knew how stressed I'd been about the tree issue and thought I could use a break and some encouragement. She was right." The two had a great time eating cake and laughing.

When Jeannie drove Annettee home, they sat in the driveway talking some more. As they sat, they noticed a man coming around the corner on a bicycle, with the tails of his red-and-black-checked flannel shirt flapping in the breeze. He rode up the driveway. Not seeing the women in the car, he got off his bike and headed to Annettee's front door. Annettee jumped out of the car and called out to him, asking what he wanted.

"I see you have a tree that needs to be cut down and removed," he said. "I could remove that tree for $65."

Annettee was stunned at the offer. She explained, "Sir, I don't have $65 right now. Maybe you could return on Friday when I get paid?"

"No problem." He said his name was Jack and mentioned that he lived in the neighborhood. He said he would come the next day and remove the tree, along with all of the remains, and return on Friday for his pay.

Jack was good to his word, at least in part. He came and cleaned up the tree. But he never returned for his money. "In fact," says Annettee, "I had never seen him before and never saw him anywhere around my neighborhood afterward."

God had rewarded her trust in a way that was, for her in her need, a true miracle.

"*L*ord, protect us!" Beverly McKinney exclaimed out loud. She and her five passengers were returning from a women's gathering. Though the weather report indicated it would be merely overcast all day, a surprise blizzard had hit while they were on the road.

Beverly concentrated hard as she tried to maneuver the car through the raging blizzard.

As they continued, the snow got heavier. After about ten miles, visibility was virtually nonexistent. "It was so bad," says Beverly, "that I could not see the hood of the car. The wipers were ineffective. I was becoming frightened since I had little experience driving in snow. I asked the ladies to pray. Turning around was not an option since

I could not see the road clearly enough to tell if any cars were coming or going, and it would be unsafe to try to go back the way we came."

Then Beverly sensed the Lord saying to her, "Look for lights."

Peering through the whiteness, Beverly saw a faint glimmer of light to the right of the car. She turned toward it and went over a bump as she got as close as she could without hitting the light.

"I stopped, got out of the car, and realized I was within just a few inches of the front steps of a ranch house," says Beverly. "I knocked on the door. All of us ladies hoped to at least be able to get word to our families of our safety."

The women were greeted warmly and welcomed into a cozy front room. They explained their situation and tried to make calls, but the phone lines were down. Since it was lunchtime, they were invited to share a meal with the family and the ranch hands.

While they were eating, the local sheriff had stopped by in his four-wheel-drive vehicle. "He was checking the ranches to see that cattle and ranch employees were safe. We asked him to notify our families and tell them we would try to get home soon," says Beverly. "He assured us that after he made his rounds of the ranches in the area he would come back and drive each of us home."

Later that afternoon, the snow cleared. The ladies looked out at the car. They noticed a small driveway that led up to the house with deep ditches on either side. "Miraculously the Lord had directed us straight up the driveway," says Beverly.

The sheriff returned, making good on his promise. He told them that there had been a bad accident at the intersection one mile ahead. The driver of a large cattle truck had become blinded by the snow and made a wrong turn; he hit a ditch and flipped his truck. Cattle were scattered across the road, and this had caused two more accidents. "We realized at that moment," says Beverly, "that if we had continued we would have been part of that mess. Instead, we were in awe of God's hand leading us to safety."

When he arrived home, Brett Smith looked gray and blank, like a computer monitor that had been turned off. As the vice president of business development for an Internet start-up company, he was usually mentally wired when he arrived home from a day in the high-tech world. But this November day in 2000 was different.

"How was your day?" asked his wife, Laura.

"Our CEO gathered the troops into the conference room after lunch," Brett spoke in a monotone. "No one was prepared for what he said. He told us that we didn't receive our next round of funding and that everyone needed to pack up personal belongings. Our doors closed today. Just like that, Laura, I'm out of work."

It took a moment for Brett's story to sink in. The company was kaput, and Brett no longer had a job. It meant a blow to his ego and a sense of emptiness in his life. It meant they no longer had an income. Laura was pregnant, and they had a two-year-old.

"Are you okay?" Laura asked.

"I think so," he replied, sinking into the sofa.

They knew the dot-com career came with risks, and any new start-up company was a bit of a gamble. Still, like most, they never believed something like this would happen to them. They had enough money to get by for a couple of months, but then what?

Brett sighed and added, "In high school I dreamed of becoming a teacher, but I never pursued it because of the low salaries. Maybe now is the time to make this career move." They sat silently pondering their situation.

The teaching idea took hold. Brett thought teaching at a college would allow him to share his business knowledge while guiding young adults to moral choices as they entered the "real world." But how would an unemployed Internet businessman with no teaching experience go about becoming a teacher at a university?

Brett called a professor friend he had kept in close contact with from his college days. He got incredible feedback from his friend. The professor felt Brett would be a gifted teacher, and he even suspected there would be an opening in the upcoming fall semester at his alma mater.

The catch? Brett didn't have a Ph.D. Most American universities do not allow anyone without a doctorate to teach in their business schools. However, this university proved to be a rare exception. The job mentioned to Brett was an "instructor" position designed for people with M.B.A.s and real-world experience. People just like Brett.

Becoming an instructor would require Brett and Laura to move from Atlanta, Georgia, a city of more than 3.5 million people, to Oxford, Ohio—population 12,000. They would have to sell their house, pay for a move, and buy a new home. They would leave the friends and family where they had lived for ten years and give up an unbeatable climate. And Brett would take an 80-percent pay cut.

"But," says Laura, "Brett would be fulfilling a childhood dream to teach, and we would be living within two hours of both sets of parents. We would be returning to our alma mater, where we met, and where so many beautiful memories were formed. And according to the Bible, it seemed more like God's will to make an impression on young people's lives than to make a lot of money."

At church the following Sunday their pastor, Father Al, gave a sermon about the gospel wherein Jesus calls his disciples. They are asked to leave their homes, their friends and family, and their possessions to follow Him and to do His will.

"Affluence," the priest said, "is a barrier to the kingdom of God."

Material possessions had been a major sticking point in the decision-making process for Laura and Brett. "We were willing to make sacrifices, but going to one-fifth of our existing income was more than a sacrifice—it was extreme!" says Laura. "We felt we were losing a lot, including the luxuries of Brett's corporate job, to follow God's plan."

The priest concluded his sermon with a short story illustrating how things might have gone when Jesus returned to heaven upon his resurrection:

> "The angels all eagerly gather around Jesus asking what His plan was to continue to spread His Kingdom on earth now that He was back in heaven.
>
> The Lord replies, 'I've assembled twelve vagrants to carry out my mission.'
>
> The angels are shocked, but don't want to insult Jesus. They plead, 'With all due respect, Lord, what if these men fail? What then?'
>
> Jesus answers, 'I have no other plans.'"

After hearing the message, Brett and Laura felt that if Jesus had enough faith in his disciples, surely He would give them what they needed to carry out the mission He had in mind for them. On Wednesday of that week, Brett received a call from the university for an interview.

Still wrestling a bit with whether to fully pursue the move, Laura went for a walk. "I was taking a walk at our neighborhood park, pushing our daughter, Maddie, in her stroller. I prayed to God for an answer to our dilemma. Should we follow what truly seemed like His call to a small town and a new humble life, or should we be less spontaneous and more responsible by earning a stable income to support ourselves, our daughter, and our unborn baby? Didn't we have a commitment as parents to provide for our children? Shouldn't we take care of ourselves by maintaining a strong enough financial position to save for the unforeseeable future?

"As my prayers and thoughts whirled through my head, a voice boomed, 'Go to Oxford!'"

Laura stopped the stroller. There was no one in sight. Laura knew that she was hearing God speak to her. She stammered, "Do you really want us to go, I mean . . ."

As soon as Laura got home, she shared her story with Brett. He believed her with a little reservation, since he hadn't gotten to hear God speaking firsthand. The next day, he was cleaning out his desk and came across one of his favorite poems, "The Road Not Taken," by Robert Frost. He put a copy in his briefcase to remind him that perhaps teaching, taking the road "less traveled," would "make all the difference."

The following week Brett went to Oxford, Ohio, for his interview. He stopped for a cup of coffee prior to his meeting. On the chalkboard of the cafe, next to sorority and fraternity letters and the joke of the day, someone had written out, in its entirety, that same Robert Frost poem.

Brett got the job.

The greatest concern of Gayle Smith's sister, Joan, was for the safety of her children. Joan and her family had recently moved back to Florida from Colorado and were renting a house with a pool. They had never had a pool before, and Joan had to devise the "pool rules." The number-one rule was, of course, "No kids in the pool unless an adult is present." Her two-year-old son, Jeffrey, had to be watched carefully because he liked to sneak out to the pool when he thought no one was watching. Joan had to put the locks high out of Jeffrey's reach on all the doors and keep them locked all of the time because of his bad habit.

One morning in the early winter, Joan went to the dentist, bringing Jeffrey along with her. When they got back home, she told him it was his naptime and that "Mommy had some medicine" and needed a nap too. As Jeffrey napped in his room, Joan dozed on the sofa in the family room.

Suddenly, Joan awoke with a start, prodded by a sharp sense of fear. She knew something was wrong. She ran to Jeffrey's room and could not find him. She searched the house, and by the time she reached the back door that led to the pool, she was frantic. A tall bar stool had been placed in front of the door and the high door lock had been opened. Joan rushed to the pool and there, floating on top of the cold winter water, was Jeffrey, fully clothed.

Joan jumped in the pool. Her clothes and shoes weighed her down. It took all her strength and energy to pull Jeffrey's body out of the deep end of the pool. He was cold, lifeless, his skin marbled white and purple. Joan started to perform CPR, then carried him inside and called 911.

She was working on him on the kitchen counter near the sink when he finally started throwing up water and showing signs of life. By the time the emergency medical rescue unit came, Jeffrey was breathing, but he still seemed dazed. He was taken to Clearwater Hospital for evaluation and observation. The doctor said they would not know for at least twenty-four hours if he would have brain damage from his near drowning. Joan and the family waited and prayed that Jeffrey would be okay.

The next morning, the word came that Jeffrey was going to be fine. It was a very close call. Joan says that the first thing Jeffrey told her when he came to was, "Mommy, I saw Jesus."

Jeffrey described a man in a white glowing robe Who came and rescued him and told him he would be okay. "We all knew it was a miracle," says Joan, "and that Jesus still works miracles today. Jeffrey is now twenty-six years old and is just as healthy as he is handsome." Joan is thankful and amazed that the Lord nudged her awake just in time.

On a snowy March morning in 2002, Rachel Wallace-Oberle read a heartbreaking story in her local newspaper of a mother whose four children died in a house fire. According to the story, the mother was believed to be at fault and alleged to have inflicted horrendous neglect. Over the next days, every detail of the allegation was exposed, and the community was outraged. The mother was reported to be suicidal and suffering from depression.

As Rachel read yet another follow-up article a week later, learning there were mornings the mother could hardly get out of bed, the words came to her, "That woman needs to be told about the love of Christ."

Says Rachel, "I continued to follow the newspaper coverage with an urgent sense that I needed to get in touch with the mother. I began to pray for her daily."

She began her search, but ran into one wall after another. The woman had moved. People who knew the woman had no idea where she had moved. City officials said they could not release the information to Rachel. Even the woman's family claimed to be unaware of where she had gone.

Finally, Rachel decided to revisit the home where the fire had taken place. It had been repaired, and someone else lived there. The new tenant told Rachel the woman had left town immediately after the fire.

Frustrated by her lack of success, as she drove home, Rachel prayed, "Lord, You will have to take care of this because I don't know what else to do."

But Rachel decided to try one more way to find the woman. She contacted the reporter who had written the stories. The reporter was on vacation, so Rachel left a voicemail. She also looked up the reporter's home phone number and left a message there.

After several days, the reporter called back. While the reporter did not know the woman's whereabouts, she could get in touch with a friend of the woman. The reporter agreed to pass Rachel's name to the friend.

"The next day, the woman's friend called me," says Rachel. "I prayed silently as we exchanged pleasantries and then explained I was hoping she could pass on a letter to the woman for me. As we talked, the Lord began to work a miracle.

"The woman's friend was also living with serious troubles and heartaches of her own. I listened for almost an hour and then told her about the love of Jesus. Through her tears over the phone, the friend accepted Christ as her Savior."

The friend promised to pass the letter on. As Rachel explained that she wanted the woman in the newspaper to know someone would be praying for her, the friend's parting words were, "You are the only one."

Rachel trembled at the awesome power of God as she hung up the phone. Each step that had seemed to be a dead end had, in fact, led her not only to one woman in desperate need of Him, but two.

$\mathcal{E}$asing onto the freeway on a balmy Sunday evening, Marilyn R. Prasow breathed a sigh of relief. The traffic was flowing smoothly, which meant she'd get to church on time for the evening service, even after stopping for gas and running a couple of errands that had, unfortunately, taken all of her cash.

"God will provide," she thought as she looked forward to the evening service ahead. The prayer time would be a great opportunity to praise God for all of His help so far, and to ask Him for help financially. As a disabled elderly woman on a very limited income, her bank account was always stretched thin. Yet she simply placed her trust in God to meet her needs.

Suddenly, traffic slowed. A big truck had spilled bales of hay across the entire four lanes of the highway. She would be late for church. She tried to stay positive as traffic was directed around the mess.

Marilyn was an hour late to service, and the ushers quietly helped her find the only seat left where she could park her walker without someone tripping over it. She nodded to the young man beside her and turned her attention to the sermon, regretting that she had missed the music.

Finally, at the end of the message, she turned to the young man and introduced herself. He smiled and nodded toward her walker, saying, "Do you need any help, ma'am?"

"No, thank you, dear," replied Marilyn. "My walker will get me down the aisle. And I'm parked right by the front door. So I'll do just fine."

"That's not what I mean," he replied. "I mean do you need help financially?"

Marilyn stared at him in mild shock. After all, this was a complete stranger. "Oh, no thank you," she replied, feeling a bit sheepish.

"Please don't be embarrassed," he said. "See, God has put this on my heart, so I want to obey Him and help you." He looked inside his wallet and made a face. "Don't seem to have much cash myself tonight but I can write you a check."

Not quite sure what to do at that point, Marilyn mumbled, "Well, okay. Thank you."

The young man wrote the check, folded it, placed it in Marilyn's hand, said "God bless you, dear," and slipped into the crowd.

Still stunned, Marilyn left the building with the check in her hand. It wasn't until she was in her car that she finally opened it. Expecting it to be made out for only a few dollars, for which she was already grateful, she was in for a big surprise. The check was made out $2,000.

"'Oh, thank You! Thank You, Jesus!' is all I could think to say," recalls Marilyn. "I don't know why or how God moved that young man's heart to do that for me. With careful budgeting and planning, it helped meet my needs for a long, long time. I am so grateful that this young man was open to God's leading even in something so amazing or sacrificial. I thank God for having me arrive late to church that night—just in time to sit by the one stranger who could do this loving deed."

*D*uring their last few weeks of living in Japan, Fernando and Jan Lovell's thirteen-year-old daughter Kiilanda (Ke-Ke), started having seizures of unknown origin. Explains Jan, "It all started when she woke up and said that she had a tingling in her left ring finger that extended to her elbow." Fernando and Jan thought their daughter had bumped her funny bone or hit a nerve in her arm while playing at school. They iced it and rubbed Ben-Gay on the area.

The next day, the tingling sensation was worse, and they took Ke-Ke to the emergency room. The doctor thought Ke-Ke just had a bruised nerve and sent the family on their way with a recommendation of ice packs and

Motrin. About a week later, on Memorial Day, Ke-Ke said that she could hardly hear out of her left ear and that conversations sounded to her as if people were covering their mouths. The next day, Ke-Ke said the tingling was better and that she wanted to go to school. While she and other students were watching *The Sound of Music* during band class, Ke-Ke had her first seizure. This began the journey of faith-building that her family traveled over the next six months.

Back in the emergency room, a battery of tests was given to Ke-Ke to try to identify the problem. All came back negative. She was discharged and sent home, but just forty minutes after they arrived home, she had another seizure. Ke-Ke was rushed back to the emergency room, and she was sent to the pediatric ward.

Ke-Ke was diagnosed with epilepsy and prescribed a large dose of medicine. By the week's end, she had begun to experience full-blown and dangerous side effects of her medication. Jan recalls, "Ke-Ke was admitted into the intensive care unit, and we watched our little girl go through hallucinations, face twitches, severe insomnia, restlessness, agitation, dangerously high blood pressure, and involuntary movements on the left side of her body, which eventually led to a complete loss of use of the left side. Still there was no clear diagnosis, no cause, and no cure."

In early June, Ke-Ke was transferred to Tripler Army Medical Center in Hawaii. There, the doctors performed another series of tests, each still yielding negative results. "We knew that the enemy was hiding himself by mimicking symptoms of other disorders to confound the medical professionals and us," explains Jan.

During this time, Ke-Ke had gone into a partially comatose state. She was having uncontrollable movements, and this eventually led to her muscles breaking down. She completely lost voluntary use of both sides of her body. Ke-Ke began to murmur to herself with periods of shouting out into the air. Her left lung had begun to collapse and a tracheotomy was performed. Still confused, the doctors had prescribed twelve different medications in order to keep her still so that her small body could rest.

By early July, Ke-Ke had so many machines and tubes for life support that a regular medical plane could not accommodate her needed power supply. She was moved to an Air Force Base for transfer to Stanford University Children's Hospital on a C-5 cargo plane. At Stanford, doctors were also baffled by her condition. They immediately stopped the paralysis-inducing drugs to see how she would respond. "Thankfully," says Jan, "as the drugs left her system, her movements became voluntary again. Within five days of arriving at Stanford most of the life-support machinery was removed."

While Fernando and Jan were convinced that God would restore their little girl, the doctors held out little hope for Ke-Ke's survival. "Within two and a half weeks, the remaining machinery was removed, her medications were again substantially reduced, and she was able to start physical therapy to relearn how to walk," declares Jan.

On July 27, Ke-Ke was transferred to pediatric rehabilitation, in San Jose, California. She was there for five months. "It was still a walk of faith," explains Jan, "but with the power of the Holy Spirit, she had even made greater recovery. She began to talk, eat regular foods, read, walk, run, and play basketball. God blessed and moved."

By mid-September, her feeding tube was removed, and Ke-Ke was fully able to enjoy a regular meal. Her medications were reduced again. "She was only having problems with her cognitive faculties," says Jan, "and fine motor activities such as tying her shoes."

After a brief setback, Ke-Ke was allowed to go home for Thanksgiving. This was her first time in their new home. "It was an exciting but emotional day," says Jan. "We had lots of food, decorated the Christmas tree, played video games, watched movies, and she played with her dogs. You could see the glory of God all over her."

In December, Ke-Ke was discharged from the hospital with lots of home care instructions. With much prayer, fasting, therapy, schooling, family support, and love, Kiilanda is doing wonderfully. "We have watched her almost spontaneous recovery, as day by day, minute by minute, God speaks and it is done," affirms Jan. "The power of prayer and intercession on the behalf of our family by the saints of God caused Him to move on His promises and keep us. After a six-and-a-half-month hospitalization, Ke-Ke has been restored to fullness, and God has given her double for her trouble."

Ke-Ke, sixteen, is fully recovered today and sings in her choir.

—by Fernando and Jan Lovell as told to Monica Cane

*I*n November 1996, Jeremy Yoder was returning from a visit to his hometown in LeMars, Iowa, to where he lived in Marshall, Minnesota. He had spent the Thanksgiving weekend with his family.

He had just crossed into Minnesota and was coming up on the city of Worthington. The area was covered with snow, but the roads were relatively clear. As he drove, his mind drifted to thoughts of his return to Marshall and his new girlfriend, Sarah. They had only been dating a few months.

Just prior to their meeting, Jeremy says, "I had resigned myself to becoming a lifelong bachelor. I had recently graduated from college, and all my friends were either married or engaged. I told the Lord I would be just fine if He wanted me to remain single for the rest of my life; if He wanted me to get married, He'd have to throw someone into my lap since I was no longer going to try. Three months after that prayer, I went on a mission trip to Russia, where He did exactly that when I met my girl-friend-to-be, Sarah."

Jeremy's attention focused back on the road. The brake lights of the van ahead of him suddenly glowed bright red. As Jeremy tapped his own brakes, he realized that the road was covered in ice. Knowing he would not be able to slow or stop in time to avoid hitting the van, he quickly decided to try to move off onto the shoulder of the road.

Says Jeremy, "I eased the steering wheel to the right, causing my front end to move in that direction. However, the ice caused my back end to slide left. Seconds later, I found myself in the terrifying position of sliding side-ways down the highway, with my driver's side door in the middle of the oncoming lane."

Just then, he spotted a woman in a white car coming straight toward him. Simultaneously, he blurted out a prayer while thinking, "I'm going to die." Without some sort of miracle, the oncoming car could not avoid crashing into him.

Jeremy could see his own terror mirrored on the face of the woman in the oncoming car. He gripped the wheel and slowly started to turn left, hoping his car would slide back into the right lane and somehow stay there and not spin back into the path of the other car. The timing would have to be precise.

Amazingly his car did slide into the right lane—just as the woman's car passed. They both stared at each other with helpless and stunned expressions, only inches away from each other. As the white car went by Jeremy, the front of his car slid back into the left lane just behind the woman's bumper, yet the two cars never touched. Jeremy's car spun around two or three times down the highway before finally coming to a stop in the ditch.

Jeremy recalls, "As I sat in that ditch gasping for breath, an image came into my mind of a huge hand reaching down, gripping my car as though it were a toy, and maneuvering it in the only way that could have saved my life."

Today, Jeremy and Sarah are married and expecting their first child. They are thankful for the highway miracle that saved Jeremy.

"Looks like we've spotted that stolen convertible!" the pilot reported as his police helicopter hovered over a street in front of a Costa Mesa bank. "But it won't be here for long."

"How come?" the dispatcher queried.

"Someone just ran from the bank and is getting into the car. He threw a bag into the back seat and . . ."

"Yes?"

"Looks like he threw something else on the passenger seat. If he robbed that bank, it just may be his gun. Now he's speeding north on Harbor in the direction of the 405. If he gets on it . . . yep, there he goes! And so do we!

Heading south. He probably hopes to reach Mexico. Better alert the California Highway Patrol."

At that same moment, Beth Ann Vorbau and her mother, Barbara Bassett, were heading out for an early dinner. They were talking about their faith in God and His blessings.

"But Mom, where did you find such an idea? Is it scriptural?"

"Oh, I can't give you chapter and verse. But, if we do have a personal relationship with God as our father, then we know it's His nature to love and bless us. And how deeply He wants us to trust Him as we pray."

"But it sounds so simplistic."

"And that, Beth, is exactly why it works!"

As Beth drove eastward toward the frontage road that parallels the I-5 freeway, she thought about what her Mom was sharing. "I always knew her to be an independent thinker," says Beth, "and pretty persistent when her mind is made up. Though I value her opinions, I don't always agree with her. So that day Mom really gave me pause to examine my own habitual approach to praying."

"But, isn't is presumptuous," Beth persisted, "to thank God for answering our prayers before we see them answered?"

"Well, if mine aren't, I ask again. And then I'm quick to thank Him again," her mother replied.

"So you keep a running list, do you?" Beth teased, trying a little humor.

"Oh, absolutely!" her mother joked back, adding, "Actually, my list is not filled with worldly specifics, like possessions or wealth. But, in addition to one constant prayer, I thank Him for what He has already promised us, an abundant life filled with guidance and provision for all our needs—blessings He already has waiting to give us. He knows my needs, so I thank Him in advance for filling them, but always according to His will and timing. You see, Beth," she paused for emphasis, "my faith is in His faithfulness. So thanking Him ahead of getting what I pray for says I trust Him to answer me however and whenever He chooses."

Her mother's little stained glass picture in her kitchen window, with the words "God gives the best to those who leave the choice to Him," came to Beth's mind.

"The way I figure it," her mother continued, "He didn't go to all the trouble He did to redeem us and then be unresponsive to our prayers."

Silence fell for a moment and then she wisely added, "You see, a request-filled prayer may just sit there for awhile; however a prayer of thanksgiving can give birth to His response."

"Mind sharing what that one constant prayer is?" Beth asked softly.

"Not at all. Every day I thank Him for protecting the lives of those I love," her hand gently touched Beth's arm, "and especially yours."

That "thank you" was about to be answered.

As the two women drove down the hill approaching the frontage road west of the I-5, they could see the overpass on which two police cars sat on each side, facing in opposite directions, their lights flashing. Suddenly, rounding the curve ahead, two more police cars careened into view, racing toward them with lights flashing and sirens blaring.

As they both wondered out loud what was going on, Beth slowed and moved farther to the right of the road.

A low-flying police helicopter swooped overhead and then they saw the lights of a convertible about a block away as it straddled the middle divider heading toward them. Beth hit the brakes and they both froze as the car came at them and roared past within inches of the left rear bumper. It seemed to be accelerating as it sped past and behind them.

"We heard a deafening blast as the car's tires slammed into the concrete curb," says Beth. "Frozen with fear, I couldn't turn to look, but Mom did and saw the driver's door fly open as the car catapulted high up into the air and plummeted over the brush-covered embankment, disappearing out of sight below."

Shaken, they cautiously made their way home, stunned and speechless.

Christian Miracles

Oddly, they saw no report in the paper or on TV of the incident for two days. Then an article appeared in the paper. Beth read it and called her mother.

"Mom, he was only thirty-four years old."

"So young? But . . . oh, no! Did you say *was*?"

"Yes, Mom. He was a parolee with a history of bank robberies. He had just stolen the car and was robbing a bank when the police helicopter that we saw heard the radio report, spotted the car, and followed it to the freeway. The article says police cars converged on every freeway ramp headed south to join in the chase. He passed three cities until he suddenly took the off-ramp ahead of us and raced onto the frontage road we were on."

"But why didn't he just stop?" her mother wondered.

"Mom, maybe he just felt trapped."

"But did he deliberately avoid us?"

"Not exactly."

"What do you mean?"

"Did you notice at the time," Beth continued, "that as he came toward us, his car gathered speed?"

"Yes, was he speeding up to get past us?"

"More likely that happened," Beth hesitated, "because he put his gun to his head . . . and fired it."

"Oh, no! How dreadful!" Beth could feel the heartache in her mother's voice.

After a moment, Beth continued, "When the police found him next to the railroad tracks, where he'd been thrown into the bushes, there was no sign of his gun so they thought the blood on his head came from the crash. They rushed him to the hospital, but he died before he could be treated."

For a long, thought-filled moment, both fell silent. They were both reflecting on how the car seemed to intentionally avoid theirs.

"So when that car passed us," her mother spoke, "he couldn't have been the one driving it."

"No, he couldn't have," replied Beth.

"But we both know Who was, don't we?"

"Yes, mom. We do, and because you thanked God ahead, your prayer for protection was honored."

They both knew it was God's unseen hand that guided the driverless car away from them that day.

When Alfredo Perez was rendered blind from a chemical splash accident at work, there was no rushing him to the doctor because there weren't any doctors close by. Besides, he had no money. Such was life for most people who lived in his remote Honduran village.

After Alfredo's accident, he couldn't see. He described his vision as moving light and shadows. He couldn't see his best friend's face anymore. There was nothing to do but continue to eke out a meager living as best he could. It was that or begging.

Not long after, a mission team from Mississippi came to Alfredo's village. They brought an eye doctor, a dentist, construction workers, gardeners, vacation Bible school workers, and more. At least half the crew consisted of young people, some in high school, some in college. The rest were an odd assortment of people seeking to share their Christian faith.

The first day, the mission teams walked the villages and watched as children and adults came out of their makeshift homes to greet the strangers. The language barrier prevented much conversation, but smiles and the passing out of trinkets were easy to communicate. The people welcomed the missionaries. They knew they brought good things. They knew they brought Jesus.

Time after time, a Honduran would take the hand of a missionary and gently tug him or her toward a hut. Several would follow. Each time, the missionary would undoubtedly be taken to a person either elderly or ill, and by gesturing, the Honduran made it known that he or she wanted the missionaries to pray. The Hondurans believed if the missionaries prayed, their family members would be healed. They had seen it happen many times.

One night, the mission group sat in a circle sharing the day's events; they were worshipping, praising, and praying. Alfredo's friend brought him to the circle. The friend explained to Brother Donald, the mission leader, that Alfredo was blind and that he wanted to be prayed for. He wanted to see. Brother Donald, who spoke Spanish, talked to Alfredo and asked him about Jesus. They prayed together.

Then Brother Donald told the group of missionaries that Alfredo wanted to see, and that he wanted them to pray for him to be healed. Alfredo sat in the center of a circle. All the missionaries, young and old, placed a hand on his shoulder and asked God for a miracle.

Afterwards Alfredo and his friend returned to the outer circle and listened while the group continued their singing and praising. The eye doctor was not there that night. He had retired early, having had a long day seeing over 400 people. But his wife was present, and she witnessed what happened to Alfredo.

After a short while, Alfredo spoke to his friend, and his friend spoke to Brother Donald. The leader announced, "Stop! Alfredo says he can see." Everyone looked at Alfredo. Brother Donald translated what Alfredo was saying. He explained that Alfredo had come in able only to see light and shadows but now he could see the people. Alfredo became excited as he described more and more things he could see, the walls, the chairs, and the faces of the missionaries. Someone handed him a Spanish Bible. Alfredo opened it up and read a Bible verse.

Alfredo had received his miracle.

The eye doctor's wife found her husband and told him of Alfredo's miracle. The doctor cocked his head and said, "Well, that's nice, but I better take a look at him tomorrow anyway." For some, only seeing is believing. For Alfredo, believing was seeing.

*C*arol McLaren and her husband, Don, were serving as missionaries in Nigeria. In February 1994, while at a medical meeting in Kenya, Don and several other conference participants came down with food poisoning. Don returned home to their isolated mission station where he was the staff pediatrician at Eku Baptist Hospital. He was soon back at work, though still a little weak.

Two weeks later, Don developed ulcers in his throat and other symptoms that were indications of Coxsackie virus, related to hepatitis. He became nauseous and slightly jaundiced. He could only swallow cold banana milkshakes and had to go on IV fluids for dehydration. After a few days, Don became worse. His coloring turned green and he collapsed. In bed he would shake violently. Don now had sepsis, a bacterial infection in the blood, in addition to his other ailments.

Carol and Dr. Tina Slusher, a pediatric intensivist working in Eku at that time, prayed for God's intervention in Don's condition. The next morning, Carol radioed their mission contact in Ibadan, Sue Wilkins. Sue began trying, unsuccessfully, to coordinate with the insurance company a special airlift for Don. By God's providence, a volunteer pediatric nurse was scheduled to fly back to the United States on Thursday evening. The nurse agreed to forgo her flight and accompany Don on his commercial flight.

"We quickly prepared for Don to leave immediately. This entailed arrangements for our two young daughters, gasoline in the midst of national petroleum crisis, and an exit visa to travel overseas," says Carol. "Once again, God provided miraculously. A missionary friend offered to take care of the girls and our dog. A Nigerian friend offered us gasoline from his private supply. Another friend went to get Don's paperwork done at the various immigration offices several hours away and it was completed in record time. We hurried off and arrived in Lagos within a few hours." In the meantime, Nick Wolfe, another short-term volunteer in Lagos, arranged for the commercial airline to allow Don and the nurse to fly to Dallas, where his parents lived, with a stop-over in London.

When they arrived in Lagos, Don was much weaker and went straight to bed. Later that evening, as he was getting ready for the flight, Carol was supporting him in the bathroom as he brushed his teeth. He looked in the mirror and quietly and calmly said, "I have never seen anyone look like this and survive."

Don completed the trip, and that weekend, a fellow missionary talked via short wave radio to a contact in Dallas to find out about Don's condition. "We were all amazed," says Carol. "The first report on Friday night was that he was not in intensive care. Later, I learned that he was to be released on Sunday to recuperate at his parents' home."

On Tuesday, as previously arranged, Carol called her in-laws from a public telephone in a small town not far from Eku. Don explained that God had healed him as he left Lagos. Within an hour after lifting off, he was able to drink some water and didn't need the IV. Soon he felt hungry for the first time in ten days and ate and drank several more times on the flight. When he arrived in Dallas, his initial lab results were very high for the virus, but his levels seemed to be going down and Don felt well.

"During the four weeks Don was in Dallas, I called him from that same public telephone, and had a perfect connection every time, which was very unusual. Soon after, Don returned to Nigeria, healthy and strong. The phone never worked again."

*S*ergio and Nan were the first friends Sue Rhodes and her husband, Mike, made after moving to a new home in Southern California. They met while all four, fairly new Christians, were serving in a ministry called Fresh Start with God.

Nan's mom, Grace, was ill. She was in her late eighties, and as she became more fragile with age, Nan took on more and more of her care giving. In March of 2001, Grace was confined to her home and bed under hospice care, and Nan moved in to take care of her during what would be her mother's last months. In the meantime, Sue, Mike, Nan, Sergio, and others prayed for Grace's salvation as well as her health.

Nan's brother, Gary, was also living with their mom. He had an injured back and could not help with any of the care because he needed help himself. Gary was not a Christian, and he was not interested in hearing his sister talk about Christ. However, Nan still tried to share about the Lord, especially with her mother.

"In May, one evening," says Sue, "I decided to spend the next day with Nan and Grace, have some breakfast, and just visit for the day."

Sue arrived the next morning with some pastries and some grapes, which turned out to be Grace's favorite. She and Nan sat next to Grace's bed, and they talked and shared stories and memories of favorite family times.

Gary was there as well that morning; he popped in and out as they talked. "It was always difficult and awkward to talk when Gary was around," says Sue. "Grace's hospital bed was actually now set up in the dining room, so we really didn't have too much privacy." Sue wanted to talk to Grace about her salvation, but Gary was intrusive.

A short time later, someone knocked on the door. Surprisingly, two people Gary used to work with had come to visit him. This was out of the ordinary as no one had visited Gary in the two years since he had become disabled and moved in with Grace. Gary and his visitors went into another room leaving Nan, Sue, and Grace finally alone.

"Nan had been sharing about a cruise she and Sergio had been on," says Sue. "They had an opportunity to share about the Lord with one of the cruise employees. The employee had told them she was always frightened that she wasn't sure what would happen if she were to die. Nan then asked, 'Mom, are you sure you know where you are going when you die?' Grace answered, 'Well, I think so.' And then Nan looked at me."

It was exactly the door they needed. Says Sue, "I truly believe that at that point the Holy Spirit really took over, and my prayer was that He would give me just the right words."

Grace listened intently and the phone rang. It was Sergio. Nan answered and explained that Grace and Sue were talking about Jesus. Sergio then called as many friends as he could think of to ask them to pray for Grace.

After Sue had finished explaining how God has given us a way to know for sure where we will spend eternity, Nan asked Grace, "Mom, would you like to know for sure? Would you like to pray now?"

"Yes, I would." Together, Sue and Nan led Grace in the sinner's prayer.

After Sue left, Grace shared with Nan, "I feel more at peace now than ever before in my life." She shared that she had no fears about dying. She felt she had already received her blessing.

Grace passed away two weeks later. Through a series of divine appointments and God-directed circumstances, Grace found Christ just before she passed into eternity.

*S*ybil Clark was a student at the University of Victoria, Canada, and living with her mother. After a long study session one night, Sybil left the library around 9:00 P.M. and headed home.

"As I drove, I was feeling so exuberant about my faith, so in love with my Savior, so grateful for God's presence in my life. I was feeling worshipful, to say the least. I had such an intense desire just to be in the house of God and worship. I knew it was late and the possibility of finding an open church was remote. Plus, most of the churches along my route through downtown Victoria weren't known for Wednesday night sessions."

Lost in thought, Sybil ended up in a mandatory right turn lane and had to turn onto an unfamiliar street. As she drove she regained her bearings: the church where her sister had recently been married was on this street.

It was a big, old, traditional, very mainline, very nonevangelical church. She didn't even imagine it would be open.

"As I got closer to the church I saw this humongous rose-colored window all lit up," says Sybil. "Then I could see that the front door was propped open. I was stunned. I slowed down and could hear music playing. As I drove slowly past the open front door, I peered in. The place was packed with people!"

Oddly, Sybil had no trouble finding a parking spot. She parked and headed into the church. "What an answer to prayer—not only did the Lord find me an open church," says Sybil, "but it was also full of worshippers. There must have been more than 400 people there. I'm sure I had the last seat available as I slipped in the back. They were all singing rousing, uplifting praise songs. I was in my glory. I joined in and sang to my heart's delight."

As things wound down, the person in the pulpit, who Sybil knew was not the pastor of the church, invited anyone who wanted to come forward for prayer. A while later, the man said that the service was over and people could depart as they liked but that anyone who wanted to stay and pray longer was welcome to come into a side room and continue to pray.

"Oh boy, I wanted to keep praying," says Sybil. "I headed for the designated prayer room. I was in a state of sheer joy. I would estimate that of the 400 or so that had packed that church, about fifteen or twenty stayed for the extra prayer. It was a wonderful experience. I didn't leave until nearly eleven. I went home jubilant."

The next morning, Sybil's mother asked her what time she had gotten in since it seemed to be quite late. Sybil told her what happened. Her mother was skeptical because she knew about the church and thought they didn't have services there like the one Sybil described.

Sybil's mother had a friend who was a member of the church, and she told her friend about Sybil's experience. The woman had been a member of the church for decades, and she assured Sybil's mother that there was no way Sybil had attended such a service in her church. They would never hold that kind of a service, and they definitely did not hold Wednesday night meetings. The woman was more than certain Sybil was mistaken, but she promised to have her husband inquire further.

The next day, the husband, after talking to various people, reported that there was no scheduled service held on the Wednesday night in question, the church had not been rented to anyone else to use, and in fact had been locked and empty all night.

What does Sybil think? "I think I had a great time worshipping with angels!"

*I*n the late-morning hours on November 12, 1947, in Greenville, Mississippi, Esther Quinn struggled to deliver her fifth baby boy, Jimmy. She had gone to the hospital the day before, but the labor had not progressed the way the doctors had hoped. Esther was not doing well. She had been in poor health most of that year, and her heart condition only made matters worse. Dr. Hirsch and his son could wait no longer. Esther needed a caesarean section. There was little time for the procedural orientation. Esther was given a spinal block and rushed into surgery.

The Hirsches were considered the best father and son team in the county. The father was referred to as

Dr. Hirsch, while everyone called his son "Dr. Jerome." Esther, a devout Christian, trusted their judgment. She knew they were skilled surgeons, respected citizens, and faithful members of their synagogue.

Esther asked if she could pray during the delivery. "Not a problem at all," said Dr. Hirsch, "we're glad to have it." However, to Esther, her prayer seemed disconnected, almost incoherent, as she drifted in and out of sleep. Two days of extensive labor had taken its toll.

A few hours later, Esther awoke with a curly-haired baby at her side. The healthy newborn weighed just over five pounds. Esther's condition was improving as well. The next morning, Dr. Hirsch came to see Esther.

After the usual questions, he said, "Esther, you've told me that you were not well educated."

Uncertain of where this was going, Esther replied, "That's right, I only made it through the sixth grade."

"Really!" Dr. Hirsch exclaimed. "Then how is it that you can speak Hebrew? In fact, you speak the most eloquent Hebrew I've ever heard."

"When did I do that?" she asked, dumfounded. She had never studied Hebrew, nor had she ever heard it spoken.

"You spoke it when you were on my operating table," Dr. Hirsch replied. "And my son and I understood every word."

"I was only trying to offer a prayer to Jesus; I don't remember what I said."

"Well, we do," replied the doctor, "My son, Jerome, copied it down. Your words were definitely in Hebrew."

Dr. Jerome moved closer to her bed and asked, "Esther, do you want to know what you said?" Esther nodded a quick yes—so did her husband, yet both looked bewildered.

Dr. Jerome held up a paper and began to read, "These are the words you spoke, Esther: 'All these years you praised your own work, daily patting yourself on the back for all those wonderful operations, never giving a thought that anyone else deserved credit. It was not you! It was me—the LORD—who gave you the knowledge. I was the one Who guided your hands in every surgery. It was I Who saved your patients. You should have praised me, for I am the LORD and Savior of all people, everywhere.'" When Jerome finished, tears were flowing everywhere.

Both doctors used every opportunity to tell their patients Esther's story and the message they received from God, explaining that it was indeed a miracle. The father was proud of his heritage and full of faith when he died two years later. After his father's death, Dr. Jerome moved to Europe to help the families who had suffered in the Holocaust.

God's divine intervention at the hospital profoundly affected the Quinns as well. Their faith in God became unshakable. In every church they attended, they served as deacons and helped many to believe in God's miraculous power. When Esther died, she was still in awe over what had happened. All of their children and nearly all of their relatives are Christians. Her husband, Jim, lives in their last family home in Boring, Oregon, where he faithfully attends Sandy Assembly of God.

—by Esther O. Quinn as told to Charles E. Harrel
on January 28, 1991

*T*n late August of 1973, Peggy Toberg, her fiancé, Jason, and his mother and father, Aurora and Lloyd, set out to picnic in the park. Friends of Aurora and Lloyd, Howard and Jenny Edwards, and their two sons joined the excursion.

The group chose a picturesque spot for barbequing, right near the river that ran through the park. Peggy, Jason, and the two Edwards boys decided to go farther upriver and, using the rafts the boys brought, do a little rafting.

"We each donned life jackets and began the trip down the churning waters," says Peggy. "I was only nineteen and was terrified of water. I wasn't a very good swimmer at all."

Peggy was tense but she wanted to be a good sport. Each time the raft bounced in rough current, Peggy held on tighter. Soon, however, the swift current eased and became serene. Peggy relaxed a little.

"It was exceptionally hot that day so the guys decided to take off their life jackets to be cooler and get a tan. They told me to do the same. I didn't want to, but they reassured me that it was safe from this point out and that the river was going to be calm from now on. Even Jason assured me it would be alright."

Hesitantly, Peggy undid her life jacket, but just as she took it off, the rafts rounded a bend and the river suddenly turned back into whitewater rapids. The lead raft snagged on the rocks. Peggy and Jason's raft hit them hard. Both rafts flipped up into the air and everyone fell into the rushing, cold water.

"I barely had time to take a normal breath," says Peggy, "let alone a sufficient one to sustain me for what was about to happen next. I was drawn deep, down to the bottom by the fast current. I learned later that Jason managed to grab the side of the raft and drifted downriver with it. But I was helpless and quickly running out of air. I struggled to get to the surface but was unable to."

Then something prompted Peggy to relax. "I thought this was it," she says. "My life flashed before my eyes, including a vision of the life Jason and I had planned that now, I felt, wouldn't happen. No wedding, no honeymoon,

Christian Miracles

no family in the future. So, I did the only thing I instinctively knew to do, and that was call out to God for help. I told Him, 'I'm in Your hands, do as You will.'"

At that moment, Peggy's lungs were bursting and she couldn't fight the instinct not to breathe any longer. She inhaled, expecting water to fill her lungs. "Peace filled my being and instead of water in my lungs, it was air I was breathing," says Peggy. "As I looked all around I could see that I was very much completely underwater. I just relaxed and let the current continue to pull me downriver. The current carried me to the surface where the water was calm again."

Peggy was able to make her way to the rocks on the edge of the river. One of the boys saw her and pulled her up out of the water. She looked around to see where Jason was.

"Jason had one shoe in his hand and was casually searching for the other. I was absolutely furious with him. I had just had the most horrendous experience of my life and here he was looking for his shoe! What he told me later, and why he was not concerned, is that he'd seen someone helping me in the river so he thought I was okay."

The rest of the day at the park was uneventful, but Peggy remained in a state of awe over her ordeal. Today, she and Jason have been married for thirty years, and, she says, "I still believe God gave me a personal miracle that day."

*S*haunna Howat, her husband, Kyle, and their two-year-old son, Tyler, moved from Phoenix to Rapid City, South Dakota, so that Kyle could take a new job and support the entire family. Shaunna had given up a job as a communications consultant to be a stay-at-home mom. She was pregnant again, and finances were very tight as they adjusted to their new situation.

When Shaunna was four months pregnant, her doctor ordered an ultrasound because he couldn't detect a heartbeat. Sadly, the ultrasound revealed the baby had died. After a brief stay in the hospital, Shaunna returned home. "It was hard to shake the deep sadness I felt. Then the doctor and hospital began calling, wanting their bills paid. We just didn't have the money to pay those bills. Finally, several calls later, the hospital insisted that somehow we needed to send them $75 a month.

"I knew I was supposed to keep relying on the Lord, even though it was hard to see His hand at all. All we needed was $75 more a month, but with things so tight, that was a lot for us." Shaunna and Kyle prayed for God to provide, and continued to endure the humiliating stream of phone calls demanding payment. Shaunna considered returning to work.

"Then I got a call from our pastor, LeRoy Flagstad, from Trinity Lutheran Church. He did not know of our problem since we hadn't shared it with many people, not even our family. He was calling because he had heard that I could write."

The pastor explained, "I need someone to spend a few hours in our office typing up and proofreading our weekly bulletin. Our secretary is just too busy, and that's one thing she'd rather not do."

As Shaunna listened, she figured he was going to ask her to volunteer. She was mentally assessing how she might manage a few hours if she could get a sitter. She was thinking that getting out of the house for a few hours a week might be a good thing.

Then she heard her pastor say, "I'm afraid I can't pay you too much. Would $75 a month be enough?"

Shaunna was stunned and filled with gratitude. "At that moment I knew that God was specifically providing for our needs. How could we ever have doubted? After all, Philippians 4:19 says, 'And He will supply all your needs, according to the riches of His glory.'"

When Shaunna was pregnant again (this time with a healthy baby girl, Kenna), the bank that employed Kyle was sold, forcing all of its employees to look for new jobs. God's earlier miracle had shown them how much He loved them and was in control, so Kyle and Shaunna trusted God with their future employment.

"When it came down to 'stay in Rapid City with no apparent job' or 'move to another city for a certain job and leave this wonderful church family,' we laid the choices before the Lord and asked Him to make it clear." Kyle fielded an offer from a bank in Michigan while Shaunna pushed worry aside and asked God to provide as He had done before.

Relying on the test of fleece as Gideon had done in Judges 6:36–40, Kyle laid a "fleece" before the Lord. "Father," he prayed, "you know what we need to live on. If this is the job You planned for us, then we know You will provide." And Kyle prayerfully decided on a salary he knew they could live on as a family of four.

When the bank in Michigan came back with a firm offer, they wanted to pay exactly what Kyle had prayed for—no more, no less. It was enough for the young family to rent a modest house and provide for their small children. They took a step of faith and moved to Michigan, to a new job. They moved again after that, with God always providing just what they needed. Throughout it all, a third child, Daniel, was born, and their first child, Tyler, graduated from high school.

*H*enry Lingley winced as the van's engine began to lose power and he felt the worried eyes of his wife, Chris, from the passenger seat. "It's starting to smoke," he heard her say. He glanced at the black twirls of smoke escaping at the edge of the hood as she added, "Do you think we should pull over?"

Henry nodded and signaled, easing onto the right shoulder of the busy highway. Keeping the engine running, Henry turned to their six children in the back seats. "Everything's fine. I just need to get out for a minute and look under the hood."

The family was returning from a weekend in Connecticut where they had celebrated Chris's mother's birthday. Their home was only a couple of hours away in Massachusetts. Despite having already been on the road an hour, they hadn't gotten far.

Henry slid back into the driver's seat. "I don't know what it is. Everything looks fine. But it could be the head gasket. We're low on oil, too." He reached under his seat where he kept extra oil. "This should do the trick," he said as he got back out of the car and poured the oil in the struggling engine.

The delay caused the kids to become restless. Henry William, age seventeen, distracted the younger ones with word games and car activities. Heather, the oldest, handed out goodies that Grandma had provided when they left. Soon, they were on their way again.

After only a short distance, there was more smoke, ebbing of power, and now the smell of burning rubber.

"Should we pull over again?" asked Chris.

Henry kept his eyes on the road. "No, I think we should just keep going. Let's just try to reach our exit so we can get off the highway as close to home as possible." They prayed all the way.

Before reaching home, they had to stop briefly at a store so that Henry could buy more oil. Hours passed before the family finally reached home. Henry pulled up in front of the house between Heather's station wagon and his own work van, turned off the key, and echoed with his family, "Thank you, Lord!"

A few days later Henry and Chris talked about what to do about the van. "We don't even have the money to pay for a tow to the shop for a diagnosis," said Henry. "I've been praying about it and I feel as though God wants us to just leave it in the driveway until we have the funds to pay for the repairs."

"What could be wrong with it? It seems rather serious," said Chris.

"I don't know. I could call Dave. He'd probably know what was up with it if I explained the things it was doing on the road."

Dave, a long-time friend, worked at an auto shop where engine work was routine procedure. He diagnosed the problem in no time and told Henry, "I know where I can get you a new engine and I'll put it in for you for, say, $1,500. Or I could rebuild it, if you'd rather that."

"Great. Thanks for your time, Dave. I'll get back to you on this." Henry shared the news with his wife. "We could start saving now, and then pay for the engine, the grill that broke last month, and the other small repairs all at once."

"So, we should shoot for $2,000?" asked Chris.

Henry nodded and the two set the need on the back burner while they resumed their lives and trusted that God would provide the funds. In the meantime, the busy family made do with the two vehicles that were working.

About a month later, Chris was in the middle of home schooling her children in math when the phone rang. The man on the other end of the line said, "I would like to speak with Mr. or Mrs. Henry Lingley, please."

"Yes, this is Mrs. Lingley." She rolled her eyes and added a superficial smile to her tone. Somehow, the telemarketers always seemed to know her class schedule.

"Good morning! I am calling from Matthew's Chevrolet GEO. Mrs. Lingley, I have a brand new Chevrolet van for you this morning, waiting just for you in the lot. All I need is your license number and this new vehicle is all yours!"

"I'm sorry, but I'd rather not give you that information over the phone. I appreciate your call, sir, though I'm really not interested in your offer. Have a wonderful day!" Chris was about to hang up, but the man urged her to take him seriously. She insisted again, "Sir, I'm really not interested."

"But ma'am, this is not a sales pitch. Someone just walked in here and bought a brand new Chevy Astro van in your name. They have requested to remain anonymous and just asked that we call you and have you come pick it up." He paused uncomfortably at the awkwardness of the situation. "I, I know this is strange, ma'am, this kind of thing certainly doesn't happen every day. I just need you to give me your license number so I can register the vehicle in your name and then it will be ready for you to pick up."

Chris blinked and thought. Hesitantly she said, "Well, can I get back to you on this?"

"That would be fine, Mrs. Lingley. Thank you for your time, and have a nice day."

Sensing something was unusual about the call, the children looked up at their mother inquisitively. "God just gave us a new van!" said an awestruck Chris, her face glowing with a surprised smile. "The car dealers said someone just walked in there and bought a new van for us!" She covered her mouth with her hand, speaking softly. "We shouldn't be this surprised at God's faithfulness to us."

Sarah spoke first, exclaiming, "We aren't surprised, Mom, we're awed! You should call Dad and tell him!" Chris agreed.

The news brought Henry right home. After a bit of discussion with Chris, he called the man from the dealership.

A short while later, the family piled into the station wagon, giggling and reliving the phone call while they rode the thirty minutes to the car dealer. Once in the parking lot, the children waited among the shiny trucks and cars while Chris and Henry went indoors to sign papers and complete the registration.

There it was, being driven up the center of the lot by one of the employees: a brand-new, teal Chevy Astro van. Eight happy people gathered around, looking it over.

Christian Miracles

Henry looked at the license plate: 2320 GG. "Isn't that interesting? Ephesians 3:20 declares God's ability to 'do exceedingly, abundantly above all we could ask or think' and only a Great God could make good on that kind of promise!"

The family began inspecting and evaluating their new blessing, praising and thanking God with every other breath. The price listed on the sticker was $27,783.00. Gadgets of comfort and convenience seemed to grace every inch of the new model.

Utter gratefulness to God fills each heart as the family feels God's intimate touch on their lives every time they ride in their miracle van.

—as told by Sarah Lingley

*L*ife had not been so kind to Carolyn Kirkman. Her husband had died. She had managed to raise her five kids alone and often took on the caretaking of a grandchild or two. That was until her heart gave out and required surgery. Later, while she was trying to clear her hayfield, a roll of tin got away from her and sliced her ankle. The injury made walking difficult from then on.

Money was tight, and Carolyn earned what she could by garage sales and clipping coupons. But there were blessings, too. Once she won a school bus–load of candy and donated it to the local elementary school. She even won a new car. The bank called one day to tell Carolyn she had won a Dodge Neon. "What's a Neon?" she asked.

Her biggest challenge lay in her house. The house where she had raised her children was falling in to the point where pigeons had set up housekeeping in the upstairs. She had learned of and applied for a housing grant. But over a year passed with no word about her application. When she visited the office she was told, "There's a long list."

Carolyn left feeling down. She had no way to pay for the repairs her house needed. Even if she got the grant, it had been over a year since she got the estimate. Prices would have gone up. But only a week later the office called and she was told, "You've been approved."

Carolyn drove to the office in happy disbelief—then she saw the check for only $5,000. They explained that Carolyn would have to contact the contractor and see if he was still interested in the job. She would have to decide how much she could have done to the house. Some things would have to wait.

That Sunday at church, Carolyn mentioned the grant and her situation to her new pastor. She had been attending a church with the kindest congregation she had ever known. They had taken her in and wanted to help. Later the pastor discussed with two men in the church what they might be able to do to help Carolyn.

"I'm not sure we can do anything," said one of the men, Richard. "This job seems too big for our church to tackle."

The other man, Jack, offered, "We could go check with the Mennonite Disaster Relief Services. I saw their truck in town."

The three men piled in a pickup and drove to the Mennonite office. On the way, Richard said, "I don't think they do stuff like this. They help with disasters."

Jack replied, "This is a disaster for Carolyn. It won't hurt to ask."

Inside the office, a man introduced himself as Herman and asked how he could be of help. The three explained Carolyn's situation. Herman listened and said, "Let me get back to you."

The next day Herman called the pastor. "We have a team of Mennonite workers coming in tomorrow for spring break. They can't do the work that we were planning because the ground is too wet. We'd like to take on your project. We'd like to help Miss Carolyn but we'd have to start this afternoon."

In a few short hours Herman met with the people at the grant office and received approval to go ahead. However, the person who managed the grants was stunned. "You are going to do this project for free?"

"Yes," said Herman. "That's what we do. Help others."

That afternoon the Mennonite team converged on Carolyn's house, which was about to get an "Extreme Makeover" of sorts. Carolyn's neighbors quickly organized to fix food for the team. Behind this team, another would be coming.

For over two weeks workers from Canada, Michigan, and Louisiana came to work on Carolyn's house. The only cost to Carolyn was for supplies. When all was said and done, the entire renovation, which included more repairs than Carolyn had originally hoped for, came in just below the $5,000 sum.

Carolyn felt like she lived in a mansion. When anyone asks about her house, she's quick to say, "It's a miracle house!"

—by Carolyn Kirkman as told to Shannon Rulé

*T*t was February 14, 2003: Valentine's Day. Not having a "special someone" in her life at the time, Vivian Batts was feeling a little down. On the way home from teaching, she purchased a floral bouquet and candles. She put the flowers and candles in the spare room that served as her office and den. She lit the candles and got busy catching up on school and personal work. "As I worked," explains Vivian, "the candles burned out, or so I thought. When I was done, I shut down my computer and went downstairs to have some dinner."

After dinner, she read the newspaper, watched television, and catnapped during commercials. Suddenly she was startled by the sound of an alarm. She was sure it wasn't due to an intruder, but she tiptoed up the stairs just in case someone was there. When she looked into the room where she had been working, flames were sprouting from the top of her file cabinet.

Instead of calling the fire department, she rushed to her bedroom to get dressed. "Never once had the thought entered my mind to douse the flame with water. I ran back to the office and moved the maple dresser away from the flames. This dresser had been in the family for as long as I've been living, so it had to be saved from potential fire and water damage."

Just then the phone rang. It was the alarm company asking if there was a problem. "No," Vivian stated matter-of-factly, "I am trying to put out a fire."

"Get out of the house now," said the security company caller. "We'll notify the fire department."

Once she was dressed, Vivian ran back downstairs. She was slowly becoming hysterical as she began to fully ascertain her situation. She opened her back door to let out the increasingly thick smoke, and then ran out of her front door to go to her neighbors, John and Sarah, and ask for baking soda to throw on the fire.

That night, the area was experiencing a severe blizzard. "It took me about two or three minutes to clear the snow from their front door to get it open," says Vivian. After Vivian finally explained to John what was happening next door, he exclaimed, "Get some water!" And Vivian shouted, "Get the baking soda!"

Meanwhile, the fire was still burning in the same spot, but the smoke was pouring downstairs. They could hear the approach of the fire trucks as they ran back to her house. Just as they arrived, the phone rang again. It was the security company telling Vivian, firmly, to leave the house. She simply informed them she had a fire to put out and hung up. She went into her kitchen and filled two pots with water. John brought the baking soda. The two of them went upstairs and doused the flames with everything they had!

Just then, the firemen arrived on the scene, came upstairs, and escorted both John and Vivian back to John's house so that the professionals could deal with the fire.

Recalling the scene, Vivian says, "In my hastiness, I left the water running in the kitchen. My kitchen floor was flooded. The fire only damaged one wall in the office, but the smoke damage was quite intense. Had I not had cathedral ceilings, the smoke damage would have been worse and would have spread downward." It was a mess, but not as bad as it could have been.

"The next evening," says Vivian, "there was a report on TV of another kitchen fire. The occupants had gotten out before the house was totally engulfed in flames. I later realized that in my case there were indeed angels in my office that night, keeping the fire at bay, in the corner. The fire did not spread—despite my fanning it by opening and closing doors. My neighbor and I were uninjured. My house was not engulfed in flames. My curtains were only slightly singed even though they were next to the flames the entire time. The only main damage was to the right side of my file cabinet, and the fire destroyed only those papers on top of the file cabinet. I am totally convinced that God dispatched His angels to protect my house and me that evening."

*A*s is their custom, Kim Rogers and her husband, John, usually volunteer at the local correctional facilities near wherever John has a pastorate. They lead Bible studies and minister to the men and women in various ways.

"There is a lot of pain and hopelessness in prisons, a lot of sadness," notes Kim. "The women always seemed sincere in their desire for Jesus and change, and it was always a disappointment when upon release, many of them have done neither. We saw quite a few of them return to prison again and again. However, there are also the few who do succeed in turning their lives around."

One morning, Kim got a call from a facility's social worker telling her that one of the pregnant girls who attended the Bible studies wanted to see Kim about taking custody of her baby until she could get her life together.

Kim was stunned. She certainly didn't want another baby. Her kids were all grown, and she had three grandchildren. Seven years ago they had adopted one "last" baby. Still, Kim agreed to see the girl anyway.

"I did everything I could to discourage Jill* in her choice of us," says Kim. "After all, she didn't really know us well at all. However, she wouldn't be swayed."

Jill was in jail for selling and using crack cocaine. She had been four months pregnant when she was arrested and already had a five-year-old daughter who had been born addicted to crack, and whom Jill's parents were raising. This time, her parents didn't want anything to do with raising another "crack baby." It was obvious that she had nowhere else to turn.

"Despite really not wanting to take on the responsibility of another baby," says Kim, "Someone opened my mouth and told this girl I'd keep her baby for a year, provided she kept her end of the bargain, which was to get out, get clean, and get it together (and my own personal prayer—get saved)!"

*Name has been changed

Kim went home and told her husband what she'd agreed to. John wasn't really happy, but since he was the one who had actually brought the last baby home, there wasn't much he could say.

As the week progressed, Kim had serious doubts about her decision. Friends and coworkers were quick to point out that she wasn't young anymore and how foolish the whole thing seemed. Some even went so far as to declare her decision "stupid." Kim felt the sting of their insensitivity, but she wondered if they were right. "Secretly, I was also calling myself stupid. What could I possibly have been thinking? As a matter of fact, first thing Monday morning I planned to call the jail and set up a meeting with Jill to tell her to find someone else."

When Kim called the jail on Monday, before she could explain her reason for calling, the social worker told her that Jill's baby had been born the night before and that they had been trying to reach Kim! She couldn't back out now.

Kim and John visited Jill in the hospital. At the end of three days, Jill was returned to jail. Kim and John took home a brand new baby girl. On Sunday morning, they brought the baby to church, and so began the work of the Lord through the life of a child named Gabrielle. That was February 2003 and the beginning of a series of miracles.

Reports Kim, "It was amazing. One of the most prejudiced couples in the church embraced this newborn baby as if she were their own grandchild. Everyone in the church loved her and cared for her, providing for her as if she were their very own beloved. Her maternal grandmother actually called and wanted to meet us and see the baby, so we went to her other granny's house to meet the family. It was such a blessing. They fell in love with little Gabrielle, and we began a family."

"Jill completed the required programs to get released from jail. She accepted Jesus, got a job, and now teaches the children in Sunday School. She's like a daughter to me," says Kim. "What a wonderful and amazing series of miracles God allowed us to participate in!"

*G*reg Outlaw had spent years living up to his name, and at the age of thirty-four he was paying a price for it. He was diagnosed with very painful advanced chronic pancreatitis for which the doctors told him there was no cure. All they could offer him was morphine to manage the pain, but that was it. Greg Outlaw was dying.

Greg's first reaction when he heard the news was to do what he'd always done. He went out and scored some more cocaine and went on a binge. What did he have to lose? His life? That was already a done deal. He may as well be comatose for what was left of it.

Later, after the drug high wore off, he began to think about his life. Something stirred deep inside him in a way he had not felt for years. Whatever it was, he was pretty sure it had something to do with God. So he called his brother-in-law, Corey, who'd been hammering him for months to go to a recovery program with him at church.

Greg had pretty much given up on God after his dad left when Greg was about twelve. His dad had been a church deacon. Every Sunday, he had taken the family to church and Sunday school in their little town in North Carolina. Then one day it was discovered that his dad wasn't the kind of man he had appeared to be. On the side, he drank and fooled around with other women. Greg was devastated, for himself and for his mother. "What kind of good God would let that happen to my mom?" he wondered. "What kind of good God would let my family be hurt like that? If there was a God, He must not be good, after all."

But now, with eternity staring him in the face, Greg decided it might be a good idea to give God another chance. He agreed to go to the recovery program with Corey. He didn't really expect much from the first session. He wasn't sure he'd feel comfortable around a bunch of "Jesus people." But what Greg found were genuine people overcoming real problems with God's help. By applying sound Christian principles, they were getting their lives back again. That night, the "something" stirring inside him grew stronger.

Greg knew he didn't have much time left, but he became determined to give whatever was left of his life to

God. For the next year and a half, he existed on morphine, for his pain, and the Bible. He read it completely through three times. His wife, Candy, and his job with an Internet company helped keep him sane. His poor health kept him home a lot, but the work was good when he could get there. He really enjoyed the challenge of changing technology.

But then Greg became aware of decisions being made by his company that he believed to be wrong and unethical. He was torn about quitting—he and his wife desperately needed the insurance his company provided. Finally, the pressure to make the choice became too great to ignore. Greg quit his job.

"As I pondered and prayed about our future," says Greg, "seeking direction for my life from God, I noticed something amazing. The pain that had been my constant companion, that had me tossing back 300 milligrams of morphine a day, vanished. Was it a fluke? There was only one way to find out. Over the next three weeks, I weaned myself off the pain-killing drug completely."

Greg began working with a ministry to develop Web sites. Eventually, Greg and a friend, Randall Niles, a former atheist, formed All About GOD Ministries and launched fifty Christian Web sites.

One year later Greg went to see his doctor—the one who thought he'd be dead by now. His doctor could not believe Greg was the same man he'd diagnosed before. Not only was Greg alive, but the formerly emaciated man, hung together by skin and bone, had filled out and looked the picture of health. Tests showed Greg to be completely free of the chronic pancreatitis condition. No pain. No morphine. No more running from God.

Today, Greg Outlaw is only running one thing—an Internet ministry that is reaching thousands of people every month. His health is fully restored, and God has indeed found a use for Greg's technology skills.

—by Greg Outlaw as told to Peggy Matthews Rose

*J*im Bell and his wife Margaret lived on a very strict budget while Jim was a student in Ireland. They cooked cabbage, turnips, and potatoes from the outdoor market on Moore Street, the downscale but colorful area in the heart of Dublin, and they lived in a small apartment with Margaret's four friends. Since Margaret's mother was their landlord, rent was only about fifteen Irish pounds a week. Margaret sold fur coats, but she received below minimum wage and relied on larger commissions from sales to keep them going. Jim focused on his studies in English, Irish, and American literature and worked on his thesis.

Some weeks, when Margaret had no large commission sales, they felt they would need to choose between paying rent or buying food. Says Jim, "Food always received higher consideration. But the Lord seemed to always provide. Though we were learning to trust Him from week to week, God was about to show us two miracles of provision at the end of our stay in Ireland that would be lessons for a lifetime."

Before traveling to Ireland, Jim and Margaret had been married in the United States with plans to honeymoon in Yugoslavia. "A cover photo on a *National Geographic* magazine I saw on my parents' coffee table drew my attention to the country," says Jim. "There was a still shimmering icy-blue lake with an island in the middle that had an onion-dome church on it. Up above it was a cliff with a beautiful castle perched on it. I was hooked."

They planned to stop off in England and stay with a friend for a few days and then take a bus to the beautiful Alps in Lake Bled. They settled in London with their good Christian friend, but the trip departed only once every week. Every week there was a problem. "The first week we were late," says Jim. "The second week I discovered as an American, I needed a special visa. The third week I went to get the visa on the only day they would accept me, but it was a special holiday and once again they were off."

Their English friend encouraged them, saying she felt the Lord would clear the way. "Give God time," she said.

By the time Jim was able to get the visa, he and Margaret needed to move on to Ireland to begin Jim's studies. They had to postpone the trip to Yugoslavia indefinitely.

"As my studies wound down in Ireland, and we were preparing to make plans to return to the United States, we had no funds to take the trip to Yugoslavia," explains Jim. "Just as we were deciding it wouldn't happen, both my sister-in-law and mother-in-law gave us belated wedding gifts in the form of cash. It was enough for the trip. We enjoyed a ride on the famous Orient Express train that was to shut down soon after. We had a marvelous time and made it back to Ireland with barely a few pounds in our pockets. Our English friend's word from God came true—it would happen in His time." They would encounter this message again in a surprising way.

Having enjoyed the amazing blessings of God in Yugoslavia, Jim rejoiced and said to Margaret, "Now I've got this faith thing down pat." What he didn't know was that their faith would be tested again very soon.

Over the next few weeks, they scheduled their flight home to the United States and tied up all the loose ends in Ireland. "We had just enough money in Irish pounds to make it work," says Jim. "We would arrive at my parents' home penniless, and I would get a job. As the day dawned on a bright Sunday morning in June we left very early for the airport because we knew we couldn't afford to miss the flight. When we got to the ticket counter, we were told that Margaret's visa had expired. She was still an Irish citizen, but because she was married to an American citizen, it was simply a matter of having it stamped at the American embassy in Dublin."

The problem was that the embassy was closed early on Sunday morning and Margaret would have to go back into the city from the airport. They were also told that the next flight with seats available wouldn't leave for another four days and would cost an additional 55 Irish pounds.

Margaret rushed back into the city by taxi and somehow got the American ambassador out of bed to stamp the visa. As she came into the airport, breathless and waving the visa, Jim sadly had to tell her it was too late; they had just missed the flight.

They left the airport and went back to an apartment they were supposed to have vacated. With virtually no money left, they'd have to live practically on bread and water for the next few days. Jim's first thought was to borrow the money from his parents or Margaret's family in Ireland. But Margaret said true faith would be to wait and let God provide miraculously. "Isn't He capable of that?" she asked.

Jim agreed, and they began the wait with the realization that as of the next morning, they only had seventy-two hours until the rebooking would expire and they would lose the entire flight. "Perhaps we could become Irish gypsies and panhandle on the streets of Dublin," Jim joked.

That afternoon Margaret called a godly little old lady friend, but she didn't tell her of their need. They used to go over for tea and scones with the woman, who seemed to have a direct pipeline to hearing from God. She told Margaret that God had spoken to her the previous evening from the Book of Isaiah, Chapter 55, and had told her to give the young couple something. She invited them to tea that night.

That evening, after some strong black Irish tea and strawberry scones, the friend shared what the Lord had spoken to her: Isaiah 55:1 states, "Is anyone thirsty? Come and drink—even if you have no money. Come, take your choice of wine or milk—it's all free."

Then she handed Jim and Margaret an envelope containing exactly 55 Irish pounds—just what they needed for the additional airfare. "She told us that the Lord wanted to give us the same amount corresponding to the chapter number in Isaiah," says Jim. "She had no idea that we needed that exact amount. The verse itself was so appropriate in terms of what God wanted to teach us. He has an endless supply to meet our needs. If we are thirsty we should come by faith and drink from His supply."

Jim and Margaret began their journey home where they would start their newlywed lives in the "real world," beyond student life, with a lesson they would never forget. "God can and will do miracles to meet our needs," says

Jim. "We watched over the years as He continued to do so, perhaps not quite so dramatically, but generously."

A short time later, when they were back in the United States, Jim and Margaret were browsing through a Christian bookstore where they encountered one final reminder of God's faithfulness to them. Jim was stunned as he looked through posters in the store. "There in front of me was a poster of that obscure Yugoslavian island and Lake Bled. But the caption on the poster was what blew me away. It said, 'Give God time.' These were the exact words of our English friend related to this exact lake."

*I*n August 1954, at age twelve, Margaret Lang came down with polio in Evanston, Illinois. This was the height of the polio outbreak, six months before the Salk vaccine came out. Just before the ambulance arrived to take her to Evanston Hospital, she heard her older brother, Dick, tell someone over the phone, "They think she has polio."

Margaret cried out, "Polio! Mother! I'll never be able to ice skate again!"

Margaret was placed in a sterile, ten-by-ten-foot glass cubicle in an upper floor of the old brick hospital, the same hospital where she had been born. "I was delirious for twenty-four hours with a fever of 106 degrees," says

Margaret. "A young intern risked infection to stay beside my bed all night and periodically wake me so that my lungs would not shut down. My father also stayed awake all night to pray for me."

A few days later, a nurse scrubbed Margaret in a tub of strong soap and sent her to a recovery ward with other polio patients. Delores Day, a physical therapist, put her through demanding daily treatments in hydrotherapy and the gym, with diathermy to relieve pain. At times when she was feeling better, Margaret would race through the hallways with the other patients in their wooden high-back wheelchairs.

"Previously, I had been an active twelve-year-old who loved to ice skate," says Margaret. "I ran with the athletic kids. After polio and six months in a wheelchair, I could no longer ice skate, and the athletic kids ran the other way when they saw me coming."

Her right plantar flexors were paralyzed. She could not bear weight, push off, or rise up on the ball of her right foot. "My gait was altered. My walking limit was about sixty feet, my standing limit was about sixty seconds, and anything beyond that caused unbearable pain and swelling in my foot," says Margaret. If she pushed too far beyond her limits, which she did from time to time, it would cost her a sleepless night of pain.

Instead of sports and running shoes, she needed Ace bandages and orthopedic shoes. To get around, she walked on her heels and supported herself on others' arms. She kneeled while cooking, and occasionally had to be carried. "I lived life mostly seated, moving from one chair to the next. Of sports, only modest swimming and short distance biking remained."

Then, in 1997, things changed when Margaret attended a Benny Hinn Miracle Service in Cleveland, Ohio.

"I was seated in the front row, first balcony, stage right of the CSU Convocation Center," says Margaret. "I had become a born-again Christian fifteen years earlier, at age forty. It had never occurred to me to ask God to heal my polio foot, as my family and I called it. It had become a part of me."

Absorbed in the worship, Margaret was startled to hear Reverend Hinn, as he pointed toward her, say, "There is a woman seated to my right who has pain, swelling, and weakness in her lower right leg and foot. God is healing you."

She was uncertain at first if he meant her, but she stood up, and holding to the railing tried to rise up and down on the ball of her right foot, while bearing most of her weight on the other foot. "It was hard but I could just barely do it," she says.

"After returning home to Huntington Beach, California," she states, "by about the third day I could rise up and push off on the ball of my right foot easily, without pain or swelling, without holding on, and without any help from the other foot. The next day, I could walk without any limp. The day after that I could run. I knew I could even ice skate if I still wanted to. At age fifty-five, I felt like a child again. Today, at age sixty-two, my right leg and foot form the strongest parts of my body. I am able to walk a mile or two a couple times a week."

The healing experience reminded her of Isaiah 40:30, 31: "Even youths will become exhausted, and young men will give up. But those who wait upon the Lord will find new strength. They will fly high on wings like eagles. They will run and not grow weary. They will walk and not faint." God works miracles for His children at any age.

"We need to get you to a doctor. Now." Robin Tompkin's friend Lisa was emphatic, her face full of concern as she examined Robin's left foot.

"A doctor? Where are we going to find a doctor out here?" asked Robin. It was Saturday. They were in Goose Island, Texas, attending a retreat for Christian women. The nearest towns that might have a doctor weren't so near, and Robin only had $10 with her.

"Don't worry. We're taking you to the doctor and that's that," replied her other friend, Danielle. "We're going back in the other room, everybody's going to pray for you, and then we're going to find you a doctor. Don't worry about a thing. We're taking care of you."

Robin and Danielle informed the other ladies of Robin's predicament, and they covered her in prayer and faith. Then the trio piled into a van and headed to a community hospital thirty minutes away.

Prior to the retreat, Robin had developed what she thought was a huge blister on the bottom of her foot. Says Robin, "I was a teacher in a private Christian school, and the week before the retreat we were taking the middle school students to a four-day science camp. I wasn't about to miss that. Middle school kids are a hoot! I loved the nights of stargazing, and watching them discovering the joys of cutting into owl pellets was pure entertainment. However, all that walking took its toll on my poor foot. I've had Type 2 diabetes for twenty-five years, but I didn't know about diabetic ulcers. I bandaged it, but continued walking on it because it didn't hurt. I was unaware of how much sensation I had lost in the nerves of my foot—also a result of the diabetes."

The worst thing that can happen to a diabetic ulcer is to have it burst, and that's what happened at the retreat. Immediately, as is typical, infection set in. The antibiotic ointment Robin had was no match for the severity of the infection. By the time she was lying on the gurney in the emergency room, she had a monster problem.

The burly blonde male nurse who first tended to her was shocked. "Whoa!" he almost whispered, "While I was a medic in Vietnam I saw all kinds of jungle infections, and this . . ." his voice trailed off as he realized he was supposed to be reassuring Robin. "The doc will be right with you." He quickly made his exit, and Robin's friends tried to reassure her.

The doctor, an intern, appeared and began examining Robin's foot. "You don't feel that at all?" he asked as he probed the wound. "That's amazing, because this infection is all the way down to the bone, ma'am. If you won't go into the hospital here, you must see your physician as soon as possible." Robin assured him she would do as instructed, and he cleaned and dressed the area. She and her friends finished the retreat asking God for a miracle healing.

Back in Houston, Robin went to her doctor as she had promised. The news was the same. "Mrs. Tompkins, this is a very bad infection," said her doctor. "We cannot treat this in our office. You need to be admitted to the hospital immediately." However, with no insurance, there was no hospital her doctor could get her admitted to. But there was one other specialist in the area with a better-equipped office, and she was referred to him.

Robin told her friends what happened, and they encouraged her. "We know we serve a God who is bigger than disease," they told her. "And you can be sure we are all praying. Don't give in to the spirit of fear; stay focused on God's Word, and His faithfulness."

The next day, Robin went to the specialist. Her situation was considered an emergency, so she was taken right in. When the specialist unwrapped her foot, Robin couldn't believe her eyes! "So much healing had already taken place," reports Robin, "the only comment the specialist made was, 'It's not so bad. We'll be able to treat this here in our office. Not to worry.'"

Robin started a regimen of whirlpool treatments and medicine. Within several weeks, her foot was totally healed. Explains Robin, "All this happened several years ago, and I haven't had another ulcer, which is another miracle, since they usually recur. All glory goes to our faithful God!"

*I*n 1979, Sybil Clark headed to Brandon, Manitoba, Canada, to attend a conference. The airport was no bigger than a large family house, with one small waiting area and one conveyor belt for luggage, and that is where Sybil stood as she waited for her bag.

"One suitcase after another came out on the conveyor belt but not mine. I told one of the airline personnel that my bag had not come off the plane. I asked the fellow if he could please quickly check the cargo hold before the plane departed and returned to Toronto, where I had just come from. They did—the bag wasn't there."

Sybil was told that her bag might have been misrouted out of Toronto. The airline worker promised that he would check and get her luggage to Brandon as soon as possible.

"It was a Sunday and a long holiday weekend," says Sybil. "I called every drugstore in town but not one was open. None would be open the next day either because of the long weekend. I had no way to get any fresh clothes, toiletries, or makeup."

The weather was warm and humid. That night, Sybil was supposed to attend a reception and needed to make herself presentable, but this would be hard to do with no fresh clothes or makeup. "My face was oily and my makeup was a mess. Desperate, I went to the yellow pages and found a woman who sold makeup at home demonstrations. She agreed to come to my hotel room and I bought a full assortment of the items I needed. But I still had dirty clothes. After she left, I was feeling frustrated and flustered. I had no nightgown, no toothbrush, no deodorant, no fresh clothes for the start of the conference the next day."

While Sybil was getting as ready as she could, the airline called her hotel room. They had not been able to locate her luggage and suspected it might have gotten rerouted to a European destination. Sybil was unhappy and discouraged. "The only One I knew Who could get me my luggage was God!" Sybil explains. "So I put in my request. I knelt down on the floor in my hotel room and talked to my Heavenly Father. I told Him even though this situation looked impossible, I was one of His kids and I knew He loved me very much. I told my Father that I trusted Him to get my luggage to me before I had to attend the conference the next morning. Keep in mind, no flights were due in until the next day, and I needed my luggage that night. I just trusted the Lord to do a miracle for me and get me that suitcase A.S.A.P."

After attending the reception that evening, Sybil returned to her hotel in a cab. The cab couldn't pull into the driveway because another car was blocking it, and a man was getting out. She recognized the manager of the Brandon airport. He opened up his trunk, took out a piece of luggage, and set it on the sidewalk.

"It was my suitcase! I got out of the cab and approached the man. He recognized me from the airport and kindly informed me that my luggage had appeared. I asked him what happened and where it had been found. He didn't know."

What the airport manager did know was that Sybil's luggage did not arrive with her on her flight; the plane and all the areas in the small Brandon airport had been thoroughly checked. No other flights had arrived since Sybil left the airport, so no additional luggage arrived.

After locking up, the man had searched the building unsuccessfully, then started cleaning up. As he was cleaning, he came into the main passenger area one last time for the night, and there sat Sybil's luggage in the middle of the room, in plain sight. It had not been there before.

"He had no clue where it came from. He had no answer at all as to how it got there. He knew how badly I wanted to get my suitcase and instead of waiting until morning to send it to me via cab, he decided to come straight from the airport and deliver it personally to me," says Sybil. "Of course I was delighted, grateful to God. The fellow that was with me, well, he could hardly believe it. He commented on my faith and my prayer and how God had really answered my prayer."

*G*randma Wakeman awoke suddenly in the middle of the night in southern Michigan. She became aware of a deep impression from God to pray for her former pastor who was serving as a missionary in the Philippines. She sensed he was in danger and she was prompted by the Holy Spirit to intercede in prayer for him.

Half a world away, it was daytime. Bob Haslam sat at his desk in the Philippine Bible College, writing furiously to create class notes for his theology class that would soon begin. He was busy with so many responsibilities that it was almost impossible to keep up with everything.

Bob was the head of the Bible College and taught a full load of classes. In addition, he was superintendent of the mission, supervisor of a major building program, and responsible for creating curriculum for extension classes for married pastors who could not attend the college. Bob was also a husband and father of two children. His duties included financial management of the college and the mission, and he was mentoring two new Filipino teachers. He was also nearing mental and physical burnout.

The Filipino superintendent of the churches begged Bob to lighten his load so he wouldn't become ill and be forced to take an emergency furlough. "Tell me what I should stop doing that I am now doing," Bob asked him. The superintendent was at a loss for words. Everything Bob was doing needed to be done, and there was no one else to share the load.

Others cautioned Bob as well, but none could help him cut back on his workload. Bob knew he was tired, but felt he had to press on no matter what. As he prepared for class that day, he forced himself to ignore his tiredness and concentrated hard on his work. "Lord, give me strength," he prayed silently. "There's no one else, and I have to keep going."

"As I sat in my office preparing for class that day," recalls Bob, "I sensed someone come into my office. I didn't look up until I had completed writing my notes. When I finally looked up, there was no one to be seen! But I knew someone had come in.

"Suddenly, I was overwhelmed by the presence of our living Lord. I felt His touch upon my spirit, my mind, and my body. I dissolved into tears of gratitude and relief as the Lord renewed me physically, spiritually, mentally, and emotionally. It was one of those divine moments when all else fades into insignificance. God took over my life with healing and enablement beyond anything I had ever experienced before."

At that same moment, on the other side of the world, the burden of prayer lifted from Grandma Wakeman as she knelt beside her bed. She got back under the covers unaware of what her prayers had accomplished.

Back in the Philippines, the bell rang for classes to change. Wonderfully renewed by God, Bob picked up his notes and headed for class. "Never had I ever been better prepared to stand before those aspiring young men and women who were preparing to become pastors and Christian education workers," he proclaims. "For days I practically walked on tiptoe with renewed physical and spiritual energy."

As Bob contemplated his experience, he was sure someone had been praying for him, and, because he knew her to be a great prayer warrior, wondered if it might have been Grandma Wakeman.

Some months later Bob was back in the United States for speaking engagements, one of which was in Michigan and his former pastorate. At the conclusion of the evening, Bob made his way to Grandma Wakeman.

"Grandma," Bob said, "have you ever prayed for me in the middle of the night?"

"Oh, yes!" she replied. "Several months ago I awoke from a deep sleep with a sense of great urgency to pray for you. I sensed you were in great danger. I wondered if you were possibly hurtling down a mountain road with your brakes gone or some other extreme situation. I prayed earnestly until suddenly the burden of prayer lifted and I knew everything was all right. Then I got back in bed and went to sleep. Were you ever in great danger?"

"Oh, Grandma," Bob replied, "I was in danger of physical and mental exhaustion and burnout. When you prayed the Lord came to me and wonderfully surrounded and filled me with His presence. He healed me and renewed me physically, spiritually, mentally, emotionally, and in every possible way. Your prayers, Grandma, kept me from collapse." Miracles of God are not restricted by time zones and distance.

*T*he summer before Sybil Clark was to start university in British Columbia, Canada, she was working in Alberta and had been reading the book *How to Live Like a King's Kid*, by Harold Hill. It was the same summer she accepted Christ and was baptized.

She had an airline reservation to fly to British Columbia that fall, but the airline went on strike and she couldn't get onto any other flights. The only other options were the bus or the train. "I loved the train ride through the mountains," says Sybil. "So I called the train station. Because of the strike, all of their sleeper cars were booked. There were, however, some coach seats left. Sitting up all night was not my idea of fun. I booked a coach seat anyway because it was sit up on either the bus or the train."

The day she was to leave she began suffering from painful menstrual cramps. The only way she found relief was by lying down perfectly still, but she would soon be on a train for hours and would only be able to sit or stand.

"I began to pray and tell my Father that I know that He loves me and that I'm one of His little children," says Sybil. "I knew my Heavenly Father who loved me so much would not want me, in such a condition, sitting up through the night and dealing with my symptoms in such a public place and in such discomfort. I asked my Father kindly if He could make a sleeper room available for His sick child. I innocently and trustingly believed that He would do this for me because He loved me. "

She arrived at the train station a little early. She had been told to ask about a sleeper when she checked in just in case someone cancelled a booking. But no one had cancelled, and all of the sleeping compartments were fully booked. The person at the check-in counter told her that when she got on the train she should ask the conductor about a sleeper. "Not discouraged, I took a seat and prayed again, trusting the Lord to answer my prayer."

When the conductor came into the coach cabin to get her ticket, Sybil told him that she was sick and asked him if there might be a sleeper cabin available. He said there was not. "After he walked away I didn't feel discouraged at all. Instead I felt excited to see how the Lord was going to answer my prayer against such odds."

Sybil also spoke with the purser who stopped to chat with her. He said he'd been offered as much as $200 by others wanting a sleeper, but there were none to be had at any price. He did mention that the train would stop in the mountains to pick up more passengers, and some of them had sleepers reserved. There was a very slim chance someone with a reservation might not make the train. Later, the purser returned and reported that, as it turned out, everyone that was supposed to board at the stop did board. Still, Sybil was not discouraged.

"I prayed again and waited. Probably another hour or so passed by. The conductor came to the coach cabin, leaned over to me, asked me if I was the young woman who was sick and wanted a sleeper for the night. I said I was. He told me to quickly pick up my things and follow him. I grabbed my belongings and followed him. We walked through one car after another until we were very close to the front of the train. He then opened a door and told me that I could have this cabin. I thanked him very much and paid him the regular rate for the sleeper room. I was so grateful to have my very own private room! God is so good. I opened my new Bible and began reading in the book of Peter. I was in my own little world of praise and worship."

Later, with her door cracked open, the purser passed by and saw Sybil in the sleeper. In shock he asked, "What are you doing in here?" Sybil explained and he was flabbergasted. He asked Sybil what she was reading.

"I took the opportunity to tell him that I was reading the Bible and thanking God for the room He'd given me. I told Him the story of my prayers throughout the day and that I had just trusted God to provide me with a room and He had. He was taken aback by my faith in God. He hadn't seen anyone pray like that and trust God like that." For the remainder of her trip, Sybil enjoyed her miraculous comfort.

Michael was a beautiful, chubby, precocious, and friendly three-year-old. He had an amazing vocabulary and magnetic personality. "While I worked as a child-care consultant for the New York City Parks Department," says Michael's mother, Robin Woods, "I sometimes left Michael at a neighborhood park playgroup. I could go to meetings without worrying about him becoming bored or cranky there. We would kiss and hug goodbye, and I would be off to my meetings."

After one such meeting, Robin walked from her office to the park to pick up her son. When she got there, she didn't see Michael. The playgroup's director informed

Robin that Michael had been picked up more than an hour before Robin arrived. Robin says, "Alarm and panic hit me. My husband at the time, Woody, worked in the field as a news videographer, and rarely could stop at home during the day. No one else had permission to take Michael, and the group's director didn't seem to recall exactly how, or with whom, Michael had left her care."

Robin ran outside and checked the toddler play area, the public bathrooms, the baseball field, and park benches. She called her husband, thinking that perhaps he had left early and picked Michael up. Woody didn't have him.

"My heart began to ache as I considered the horrible situation," says Robin. "Where could a three-year-old be in busy, midtown Manhattan? My next call was to the local police precinct. Officers were on the scene in minutes. Soon after that, Woody arrived as well."

As officers walked Robin back to their apartment a few blocks away, she stopped neighbors and strangers, asking if they had seen Michael. Less than three feet tall, he would have stood out, walking without adult supervision in this busy area. The supervisor of her building had heard the police call on his scanner and started a phone chain. He called all doormen in the immediate area, and asked them to keep a lookout for Michael. "Even utility workers offered to use their truck to search for our son," says Robin. "Woody went along with them carrying photos of Michael."

Two hours had passed, and there was still no sign of Michael. The neighborhood was buzzing with volunteers scouring the area. Police officers searched apartment buildings and rooftops for blocks around. "I ran back and forth from home to park," says Robin, "hoping that Michael had been hiding somewhere, afraid to come out. By now, he had missed lunch and his afternoon nap. I wondered if he was as terrified as we were." They had contacted their church and a prayer chain had been activated with dozens of people praying for Michael and his well-being.

Woody and Robin completed one more trip from the park to their apartment. A detective asked Woody for more photos of Michael and Woody took him inside to get more. "Suddenly, the walkie-talkie near me squawked to life," says Robin. "I overheard something that sounded like 'Child found.' Moments later, Woody came outside, our son in his arms. Michael was a very tired, filthy boy, tied up in a child's jump rope. Woody and the officer both had tears in their eyes."

Woody and the officer had found Michael curled up and sound asleep on the welcome mat outside of Robin and Woody's apartment door. They took Michael to the hospital to be examined. He was dirty, dehydrated, and hungry, but otherwise unharmed. He began chatting away happily with a detective, whom he called Inspector Gadget. He was delighted by the gift of the officer's cap, and asked for lunch and his "moofie" (pacifier). Dr. Chen, the pediatrician, assured Robin and Woody that all Michael needed was some food, liquids, and a good night's sleep.

"We have never been able to find out exactly what had occurred that day," says Robin. "At three years old, Michael couldn't explain things as well as we would have liked. We don't know where the jump rope came from or why he was tied up in it. We don't know how he got back to our apartment unnoticed by police and search crews."

All Michael said that day to Robin was, "Where were you, Mommy? I looked for you and couldn't see you. After a long time, a man came out of the sky and took my hand. He said that he would lead me home to my Mommy and Daddy. We crossed the street and I came back."

Says Robin, "Our family was the recipient of a miracle that day. I can only surmise Whose hand it was that guided Michael back to us. Whether through divine or mortal intervention, our three-year-old found his way back home. He had an angel on his shoulder that day, and I am in awe of the power of prayer and love."

One balmy summer afternoon, Barrett and Thomas Oberle, ages nine and six, decided to go biking with a friend. Their mother, Rachel, told the boys to be careful as they rushed off shouting "Goodbye" and "I love you" over their shoulders.

Rachel returned to her chores and got lost in her housework. "Gradually I became aware they had been gone for a long time, which was unusual; we live in a small town, and bike rides for the boys usually last only fifteen or twenty minutes. I had no way of knowing where they were. I began to worry." Stories of child abductions filled her mind as a sense of helplessness began to overcome her.

She was uncertain as to what to do. Then Rachel heard God's voice: "Pray."

"In my fretful state, I was incapable of formulating anything flowery; I just paced and whispered, 'Oh Lord, please put your angels around them. Please bring them home safely.'"

Hours passed. Despite her prayers, Rachel's panic grew. Her hands shook. Her stomach cramped. "Irrational snapshots of funerals and a future without my children loomed before me. The need to throw myself into my Father's arms was overwhelming. I kneeled at the living room couch and poured out my anguish. 'Where are they, God?' I cried in desperation.

"I clung to Him and within that haven of comfort reserved especially for mothers," she explained. "He wrapped a blanket of peace around me. Its warmth steadied and soothed my trembling hands. My thoughts cleared. Somehow, still praying, I managed to make it through the afternoon. As the dinner hour approached, the phone rang. I grabbed it."

"Hi, Mom," Barrett said in a small voice.

"Where are you?" Rachel asked, weak with relief.

"We're at Grammie's house," he replied.

"No, you're not!" Rachel exclaimed in disbelief. Grammie lived in the city of Waterloo, Ontario—twenty minutes away by car. The highway from their town, Elmira, into Waterloo is one of the busiest in the region.

"Yes, we are," Barrett said and began to cry.

Rachel hung up the phone and rushed out the door. She hurried as fast as she could to reach them. When she got to Grammie's and heard their adventure, the urgency to pray took on new significance.

The two boys and their friend had bicycled almost halfway to Waterloo. Barrett and Thomas knew this was too far to go, but it was a beautiful day and, well, they were little boys. At this point, their friend remembered he had a newspaper route to take care of and rushed off toward home. Barrett and Thomas lagged behind, lost their bearings, and had no idea of how to get home. They decided the only thing they could do was go on to the city and find Grammie's house; Barrett was sure he knew the way.

The two of them headed off down Highway 85 with its speeding drivers, traffic congestion, and accidents. They stopped off at a mall and went in to fill up their water bottles and use the washroom. By then, rush hour had started. Passing several on and off ramps to the expressway, they negotiated numerous sets of traffic lights and busy intersections before proceeding down the main street in Waterloo. After pedaling down side streets and up a hill, they finally ended up at Grammie's house. She was just getting into her car to leave for work as the boys appeared, exhausted and sweating, in her driveway.

"Does your mother know you're here?" she asked in astonishment.

They both shook their heads silently. The enormity of what they had just done began settling upon them. Tears rolled down Barrett's grimy face.

"One more second and I wouldn't have been here, darlings," Grammie said as she hugged them. "What would you have done?"

"We would have turned around and gone home again," Barrett blubbered.

On the way home from Grammie's, Rachel told the boys that God had instructed her to pray for them and that she hadn't stopped until the phone rang. Barrett looked at his mother in awe and said, "After we filled up our water bottles and were on our way to Grammie's, something kept telling me to hurry. I kept hearing it over and over again in my head, 'Hurry, hurry, hurry.'"

"Do you know Who that was?" Rachel asked him.

He nodded. "It was God."

Wide-eyed, the boys watched the scenery pass as they drove home. They sat close together, small and silent, as their bikes banged and rattled in the trunk.

Barrett has never forgotten the sound of God's voice that day or the power of a mother's prayers. Says Rachel, "The experience, I am sure, will stay with him for the rest of his life as shining, vivid proof that God is real and prayer works."

On June 23, 2001, Ann Hite's brother-in-law and friend, Joe Hite, died of a heart attack. Her husband, Jack, asked Ann to write a remembrance of Joe for the funeral. Reluctantly, she agreed.

Says Ann, "I sat in front of my computer without a clue, panic spreading through me. Why in the world had I agreed to something so hard, so personal? A voice told me to put myself in my husband's shoes and write in his voice. I wrote a letter entitled, simply, 'Dear Brother.'"

Although the grief of loss continued to hang over Ann, she felt she had somehow found herself in her writing. "In just over three months I had written more than I had in my entire lifetime," she says.

At the same time, with a changing economy and other circumstances, money tightened up, and by January things were looking dimmer.

"We couldn't meet our bills or buy enough food every week. My stepson had moved in permanently, and our landlord had raised the rent by $100 a month. I had begun to feel as if God had abandoned me."

Later that evening, as she stood on her front porch, a woman jogged past her house. As she made the loop to circle back, she cut across the yard and approached Ann.

"Please don't think I'm crazy, but you're a Christian, right?" the woman said. Ann nodded. "Every day I run through here. For the last two weeks, I have felt driven to stop. Today when I saw you, the feeling was so strong, I couldn't fight it any longer. God has a message for you. He wants you to know He hears your prayers and He has not forsaken you. He knows you're in financial trouble. He knows what you need. You must trust Him. He wants you to know it will not always be this way. You're making all the right decisions. Keep at it."

Ann was amazed and encouraged by the stranger's words. She stared with tears in her eyes as the woman jogged away. She would need that encouragement more than she knew.

Over the next year, their car needed repair. Her estranged mother, who had beaten Ann as a child, fell ill and needed transportation back and forth to treatments for her renal kidney failure.

"Our budget was averaging about $100 short of what we really needed," says Ann. "We needed $700 just to get caught up. At the same time, the company I worked for was placed on the market, and rumors went around that there would be no pay raises."

Still, Ann was determined to trust God. Over and over, her mind went back to the words of encouragement the jogger had shared. She was encouraged just enough to go ahead and ask for a raise at work. And then she prayed harder.

Then one day her boss called her into his office. "He told me he had approved a twelve-percent raise," says Ann. "My head began to hum. How could this happen? He also informed me I would be receiving a bonus of $900! When I left his office, my head was spinning. I went outside and did the math. After taxes and deductions, we'd have $80 more than what we needed to catch up. I could now even buy a birthday present for my stepson."

As she drove home that evening, Ann wished aloud that she could share the good news of her situation with the woman, but she had not seen her for over a year. But as she pulled into her driveway, there was the stranger, jogging down the street!

"I ran, yelling, down my front yard," says Ann. "She smiled to see me. I told her all that had happened in the year. I told her of the miracle. She smiled. Then, for no earthly reason, I told her of my writing and how I had a

Christian Miracles

passion for words. How I was sure I was meant to use my talent. She asked if we could pray. Normally, I would have felt funny praying in my front yard with a woman I didn't know, but I jumped at the chance. She took my hands in hers and prayed concerning my writing."

Later that year, after things settled more, Ann wrote ten short stories in ten weeks and submitted them to publications that fall. "By October, my first piece of writing was accepted for publication, followed by an acceptance once every two or three weeks. Over the next nine months, I had fifteen stories accepted for publication. And I've finished a third and final draft of my first novel." What were Ann's miracles? The first was hearing a word of encouragement from a stranger. The second was believing that her God would take care of her.

*D*onna Norton's son, Micah Daniel, was born January 27, 1991 with several birth defects that became apparent in just two days.

The first problem to surface was blocked urethra tubes. "His urine was filled with blood," says Donna. "He was immediately transferred to Riley Children's Hospital in Indianapolis."

As the doctors treated Micah's urethra tubes, they discovered additional problems. His right kidney was damaged, and his left kidney was badly swollen. At first, his damaged kidney looked like it had a tumor. The doctor's stabilized Micah and began strategizing surgery.

Two days later, doctors discovered a large hole in Micah's heart, a condition called atrial septal defect, or ASD. Then, doctors found Micah had a nutritional/enzyme defect known as an L-Carnitine deficiency. This last condition had the potential to cause sudden infant death syndrome, and it would severely restrict his diet and what he was able to digest. Children born with an L-Carnitine deficiency seldom live through their teen years.

When Micah was just ten days old, he underwent surgery to correct some of his urinary problems. The complications from the surgery left him highly susceptible to infections for several months, until he could have additional surgery.

Micah pulled through the surgery, but then when he was three months old, he developed RSP, a severe respiratory virus, and he was again taken to the hospital. The doctors told Donna that the best-case scenario was that Micah would have permanent damage to the lining of his lungs and he would probably have asthma for the rest of his life. Donna says, "He had to take ventalin treatments three times a day, L-Carnitine twice a day, antibiotics once a day, and he needed constant care. He was not allowed to cry because whenever he did, he would get clammy and cold from his heart condition—so we had to always keep him happy. Luckily, this was not hard to do, because Micah was the best baby I have ever seen or known. He literally was angelic—like he was touched by God."

At home, during the day, Donna often watched Benny Hinn's program for encouragement. One day, the program was on as Donna was talking to her sister on the phone. Micah, who had been standing and holding onto the couch, suddenly fell backward. Donna dropped the phone and rushed to him. "He was lying flat on his back on the floor and looking up and smiling," says Donna. Seeing he was unhurt, Donna picked up the phone and told her sister what had happened.

Just then, Donna heard the beep of call waiting. She said goodbye to her sister and answered the new call. It was her friend, Karen.

"Karen asked me if Micah had a heart murmur. I told her, 'You know he does, why are you asking?' She explained that I had never called it a murmur before but had always called it ASD and she didn't know if it was the same thing. I assured her that it was and asked her why she was asking. She said that she had been watching Benny Hinn and that he had just called out a healing for a small child with a heart murmur, and that some voice kept whispering in her ear, 'Micah, Micah,' so she prayed for him but she didn't know if that was really what he had."

Donna was stunned. She told Karen that Micah had fallen to the floor, unhurt, during the show.

Soon after this, Donna took Micah in for tests for his heart. She was shocked when doctors told her his heart looked fine. For the next few months, Micah was subjected to testing and retesting for all of his conditions, and was found to be healthy by all of his doctors. He no longer had an L-Carnitine deficiency—his body miraculously started producing it.

The only condition left, the urinary tube defect, was easily corrected with surgery. He was even released two days earlier than anticipated.

But that wasn't the end of the miracles, and they weren't all for Micah.

In the recovery room bed next to Micah lay a six-month-old boy suffering from a terminal brain tumor. His mother, Candy, sat nearby. Donna says, "It was heart-wrenching talking to his mother. I asked her if she would mind if I prayed for her and her son. She looked hesitant, but said okay." When doctors came to take new X rays of the baby boy, they found that the tumor was gone. "Candy saw us as we were getting ready to take Micah home and came running down the hallway exclaiming, 'My baby's not going to die! My baby's not going to die!'"

Before leaving the hospital with Micah, Donna shared Christ with Candy and led her in the sinner's prayer. Candy accepted Christ as her Savior.

Today, Micah is thirteen, and he has no conscious memory of his birth defects. Donna adds, "But I've told him that the scar on his tummy is where Jesus healed him. I have determined through it all that God knows best, and I trust Him with my life and the lives of my children."

It was June 1998, the summer before Serena Haneline would graduate from college, and she was desperately searching for an internship that would fit her journalism major. She didn't want to work at a newspaper, so she applied to two Christian magazine companies, Vox Corp, Inc., and *CCM Magazine*, as well as the International Mission Board, which is affiliated with the Southern Baptist denomination. She really wanted to go to the mission board in Richmond, Virginia, because she had attended a Southern Baptist church in her hometown of Kannapolis, North Carolina, and thought it would be fun to intern at a place that dealt with missions.

A rejection letter arrived from *CCM Magazine*. Then a call came from Vox Corp, Inc., a Christian company located in Nashville, Tennessee, that produced three music-related magazines and one worship magazine. The editor interviewed Serena over the phone. But Serena was still waiting to hear from the International Mission Board, the place she really wanted to go. Still, she didn't close the door. She told the editor that she would get back to him.

That very weekend a letter came in the mail—a rejection letter from the International Mission Board. Serena was disappointed, and she now had a decision to make. She talked it over with her mom. "Mom, I don't know what to do. It's all the way in Nashville. That's seven hours away! And I don't even know how I'll get there."

"You should go," her mother said. "You may never have another opportunity like this."

Serena called the editor at Vox and said she would take the internship. Then she discovered that another girl from her college, named Lauren, would be an intern at the very same place.

Serena didn't know Lauren because they were in different years. However, they were both religion and journalism majors. Serena talked to Lauren on the phone about a week before she was to leave for Nashville, and they agreed to meet once Lauren arrived.

Serena loaded her 1987 Honda Civic with all she would need for the two and a half months in Nashville.

She tracked down a friend who had graduated from her college the year before and who was now living in Nashville. The friend agreed to put her up for up to two weeks while she searched for housing.

Says Serena, "I didn't have the money to make the trip to Nashville, let alone rent an apartment. My mom couldn't afford to give me any money either. The internship was unpaid, so I would have to find a part-time job on top of everything else." Serena was walking in total faith.

On a Sunday, the day before she was to leave, Serena and her mom went to her church, Memorial Baptist. It was Serena's day to perform the special music. After she sang, she decided to let her church family know her plans. So she told them that she was going to Nashville for an internship and she didn't know how she would even get there, but she knew that was where the Lord was leading her so He would provide. All Serena expected was their prayers.

After the service, to Serena's complete surprise, members of the congregation started coming up and putting money in her hands as they wished her well. One little old lady, whom Serena didn't even know at the time, came up and laid a blue folded piece of paper in her hands.

Later, as Serena and her mom counted out the money, they were stunned. In addition to around $500 in cash, the blue paper was actually a check made out for $500.

With the abundant help from her congregation, Serena made it to Nashville to stay with her friend. When Lauren arrived, she called Serena. It turned out Lauren's parents had arranged for a place for Lauren to stay, but somehow Lauren's name had made it onto a list of students needing housing. Two people had already called her offering her a place to stay. Lauren gave their numbers to Serena.

Serena called one of the women, Kris, who lived on the north end of the city near Vox. Kris was single, in her forties, and had just moved from Knoxville, Tennessee. "She was only going to charge me half utilities for an empty bedroom with full use of everything else in the house. I took it right away," says Serena.

After sealing the deal with Kris, Serena headed back to her friend's house. First, she stopped just down the street at a drugstore to buy some postcards. While she was in there, she decided to ask for a job application.

The next day, Serena went back to the drugstore, expecting to drop off the completed application. The manager asked her to come up and talk with him. She was not prepared for an interview, wearing just a T-shirt and shorts. But three days later she started her part-time job working from four until nine, which worked perfectly with her internship hours of ten until three.

"The money God had provided lasted right up until I got my first paycheck," says Serena. "What I earned covered my expenses during my full internship. While in Nashville, I learned a lot about Christian music and the magazine industry, as well as God's daily provisions."

A homesick native of Ireland, Margaret Bell hadn't been able to return to the island for many years, primarily due to lack of finances and responsibilities to kids. Things had a habit of getting in the way of her hankering to smell the turf burning in the fireplace with a brewing teakettle hanging over it.

As family life continued in the States, thoughts of the country with forty shades of green brought back memories from her childhood of her working in the general store in the highest village in Ireland. There was no television there in the late 1950s, and most people traveled on bicycles. To the Celtic temperament then as now, God was present everywhere. God is even mentioned in the Irish-language version of "Hello" and "Goodbye."

Margaret longed to wind down with her sister and worry about nothing more than avoiding the few sheep that wandered over country lanes as she motored along.

She deeply missed her relatives and needed a break after a year during which she and husband Jim had not taken a vacation and she had a heavy workload.

"I was recovering from my fourth hip replacement," says Jim, "and she was having to wait on me hand and foot. We had an older daughter on her own, but two were still in college, and a fourth Margaret was homeschooling. Phone calls to Ireland were just not cutting it, and trips to forest preserve lakes or walks in the woods were bringing diminishing returns.

"She wasn't going to try to borrow any money or nag me to go," Jim continues. "She was going to go to the only source there is Who can transcend both these obstacles—God Himself. I remember a similar crisis period when her nerves were totally frayed nearly twenty years earlier. She was sitting in the middle of the stairs crying—and believe me, she's a mountain woman, made of steel—having just had our third child, Brigit, and was babysitting five other wee ones. I didn't know what to do at the time because I was out of a job and couldn't send her but I knew she was overdue. That time, she eventually got back to Ireland in an indirect way, but it took a while."

Margaret is a woman of strong faith and believes in God's power to directly intervene in her family's life, even to provide them the little, inconsequential things. This second time of intense longing for her home, she got down on her knees in the middle of the room one evening and asked God to reveal Himself and do a miracle by having someone provide a way for her to go to Ireland. This time, she wanted to muster enough faith so she could receive a prompt answer. Her faith had grown in the previous twenty years, and she wanted to put it into action. When she got up from her knees, she was exhausted from crying but had a sense that God heard her.

Fewer than three hours later the phone rang. It was a call from a woman Margaret had never met. She almost didn't take the phone call because she's constantly hearing from relations who have a mutual Aunt So-and-So from County Limerick. But more than that, Ireland was a sensitive subject, and she was still exhausted from crying a few hours earlier. Little did she know that she was about to experience a miracle in the works.

"This woman had met my son Brendan at summer camp," explains Jim. "Brendan had raved about his charming and humorous Irish mother. The woman asked for her phone number and called Margaret. She ran a travel agency that sent people to Ireland on tours, and she needed a tour guide who was authentically Irish."

The woman told Margaret she would send her, all expenses paid, to guide a tour for eight days all over the country—and make her family home stops along the tour route. She wouldn't need any experience but just needed to recount her knowledge from childhood. Margaret didn't need to think for very long. She was also able to bring their ten-year-old daughter, Brigit, along as well. Brigit got to meet her cousins while Margaret signed up some friends for the tour, and even wound up having her childhood friend sing for the group while they were there.

"But that's not the end of the story," says Jim. "After Margaret was about halfway through the tour in Ireland, the husband of one of her friends, who was also on the tour, casually asked me if I would like to hop on a plane the next day to Ireland and surprise our wives. How could I pass on that offer? We arrived shortly thereafter and I completely surprised her in her hotel room in Cashel, County Tipperary.

"She was a bit overwhelmed frankly," says Jim. "My friend Joe and I joined the tour for a couple days, journeyed to some unforgettable places with the ladies, and left before the tour completed. All in all, God greatly exceeded her expectations. He didn't provide for just a trip but gave her friends on both sides of the Atlantic, her child's visit, and a surprise visit from her husband. This miracle happened because it was based on great expectations of a great God."

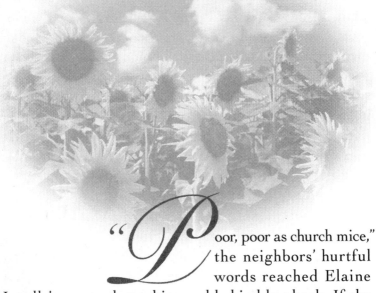

"Poor, poor as church mice," the neighbors' hurtful words reached Elaine Ingalls' ears as they whispered behind her back. If she looked at the family's material accumulations, then she would have to agree—they didn't have much.

When Elaine was about eight years old, her father had an accident that would change her life. No longer would the family live in their island home where the light from Ross's Island circled through her bedroom window and swept its path of light around the wall of her bedroom. Never again would she travel from their backyard, past the well, to open the white picket fence and follow the well-worn path to her grandmother's house.

Everything changed the day her father fell off a ladder while installing the outside windows on the house. He was in a full cast for months, and when he was finally able to walk again, the pain in his leg wouldn't allow him to continue working at the fisherman's co-op. Relatives stopped by their house on their way home from the boats with fresh fish. Her mother, Audrey, baked mounds of bread in large juice cans, and Elaine and her brothers wore their cousins' hand-me-downs, all marks of poverty. The outcome of the accident meant the family was forced to move to the mainland so that her father could find work.

Elaine recalls, "One outstanding memory from my childhood was the day my mother went to the cupboard and, except for a handful of macaroni, it was bare. No bread, no cereal, no potatoes were left to fill our empty tummies—just a handful of macaroni and no money in the house to buy more until payday."

Instead of her mother telling the children that there wasn't enough to eat, she gathered the three of them around her lap and as they held hands, she bowed her head and told God her needs. "God, You see Your children and You know we're hungry but You said You'd supply our needs. Thank You for what You're going to bring us," she prayed.

When she had finished, Elaine and her nine-year-old brother, Norman, went to their room. "Is God coming here?" Norman whispered.

"No, silly," Elaine told him in her most knowledgeable big-sister voice.

"Well, who's going to bring us our supper?" Norman was growing fast and he was always hungry.

"I don't know. Mom says God's going to supply our needs, but I don't know how that's going to happen. I know one thing though; if we don't get help soon we're going to be really hungry. I was looking in the cupboards and there's nothing in them except a half a bag of macaroni."

Suppertime came and Audrey called the family to the table. "It's not much," she said as she began to divide the meager rations into the five bowls. Before she finished spooning out the food, a knock came from the door. She slid the macaroni back in the pot and went to answer it. "Mrs. Rice!" she exclaimed. "Come in." Mrs. Rice cooked for Bethany, a Bible school located a few blocks away from the Ingalls' home. Elaine recalls that when she heard her mother's cheery invitation, she groaned.

"Here we were, sitting around the table with hardly anything to eat, and my mother was inviting someone in to share our supper! I had visions of the plain white macaroni being divided into six bowls now."

"No, I won't stay," Mrs. Rice said. "I came to bring you this pot of soup. The students have already had their supper and this was left over. They won't thank me to offer them soup again tomorrow." Audrey thanked her and returned to the supper table where the children were sitting, waiting for their dad to say Grace. She then deftly added the macaroni to the soup, making enough to feed her family until payday. "Our mother was a woman of faith and we had witnessed just one of the many answers to her prayers," Elaine said.

Yet providing for the family remained a struggle for Elaine's parents, and there came a time in their lives when her mother's prayer requests seemed too big for even God to answer. "Dad had worked for a while, but due to cutbacks, the job finished and work was scarce in the small community where we lived. After many prayers, God provided a job but my parents didn't have the money they needed to move us to the city where the job was located. Although we had no car or savings bonds to use as collateral for a loan, Mother applied to the bank anyway. 'We need to keep the family together,' she said by way of explanation. 'And we need to move to where the job is located.'"

A few days after Audrey visited the bank, the loans officer paid a visit to their home to see if there was anything worth putting on the form as collateral for the loan. "So you have no car," he said as he looked over his papers. "Do you own your stove and fridge?"

"No, it's our neighbors'. They left it here when they rented us the house," she explained.

"What about china, a television, or other appliances?" a frown crossed the banker's face.

"We have a radio," Norman exclaimed. He had been sitting at the kitchen table making a boat from a cracker box. Every night the children were allowed to take the brown radio, smaller than a breadbox, to their shared bedroom and listen to the programs before going to sleep.

The loans officer frowned. "So this is all you have?" he said, waiting for Audrey to add to his list. "A set of bunk beds, a radio, one chrome table and chair set, a double bed, and a wooden desk—no car, no home, no library . . ."

Elaine says, "My heart went out to my mother as I saw her face turn red with embarrassment."

"That's all," Audrey said in a whisper.

The bank official continued, "And you say you need $200 to pay your expenses to move to the city where your husband has been promised a job?" Audrey nodded. "Mrs. Ingalls, I'm sorry, but you must realize banks can't operate like that. There's nothing here for us to sell if you don't keep up your payments." Then, seeing the disappointment on her face, he added, "All I can do is fill out this form for you and see what happens."

Elaine remembers watching this from the kitchen. She was thirteen and very aware of her parents' struggle to provide the basics for their family. From where she stood by the stove, she could see the banker seated at her mother's desk. He stopped writing and shuffled his papers.

When he stopped, he seemed to be looking at something on the corner of the desk. At last he cleared his throat, pointed, and spoke, "Do you believe that verse?"

Audrey looked where he was pointing, "Yes, I do," she said proudly. "It's my life's motto."

"Oh." He sat there and studied the papers for a long time. Then he stacked them up and put them in his briefcase. "Mrs. Ingalls," he said as he stood by the door on his way out, "I guess I have no choice but to recommend you for the loan. Your life's motto comes with an excellent reference for your character."

Several weeks later the family learned that the bank had approved the loan and they were able to move.

What were the words of her mother's motto? "They were taken from an old hymn by Rhea F. Miller," Elaine says: "'I'd rather have Jesus than houses or lands. I'd rather be led by His nail-pierced hand.'" In the mind of the loan officer, having God in their corner provided a lot more security than a refrigerator or radio ever could have.

 early every year Luciano A. Pimentel's father, John, developed kidney stones. He would suffer excruciating pain until he was able to pass them. And he regarded this as fortunate—many of his friends had to have surgery to remove their kidney stones.

In September 1991, John had an especially bad round of stones. "We found out later," says Luciano, "that he passed one of the biggest stones he'd ever had. He was in terrible pain for hours and hours.

"Then, my mother, Adelina, prayed fervently that God would touch Dad. She prayed that the stones he was suffering from would pass soon, and that he would never again be afflicted with the problem. As she prayed, Mom felt compelled to put her hands on Dad. He was laying face-down on their bed, squirming and writhing in pain."

Within minutes after his wife's prayer, John got up and went to the bathroom. Painfully, but finally, the large stone passed, and relief washed over him.

Says Luciano, "Since that day, Dad has never again had a kidney stone. Not a single one, and this without changing his diet one bit. The Lord Jesus Christ heard Mother's prayer and granted him a permanent cure."

*A*nnettee Budzban nervously looked around the table at the other parents, some in pairs, some alone as she was. It was what was called a "Tough Love" meeting. Annettee had come, hesitantly, on the advice of a friend. Her friend thought that a support group would help Annettee, a single parent of three teenage boys, find strength and encouragement, as well as reveal some options for dealing with hard issues.

Says Annettee, "As each parent started to tell their story, I was thinking about how it would soon be my turn to speak. What would I say?"

Forefront on her mind was her son Tim, who had been through an ordeal with drugs. "I thought this demon was well behind us. Then I started picking up on hints of the problem resurfacing. We started getting a lot of suspicious phone calls for Tim. Several times a day, the phone would ring with unfamiliar people requesting to speak with Tim. When I asked them who they were, they simply responded that they were the friend of a friend. When I confronted Tim with this issue, he just shrugged it off like it wasn't a big deal. I needed some clear evidence to get him to confront his own problem."

Annettee prayed for direction from God and help in getting some clear evidence about what Tim was up to. While she felt certain it was drugs, she didn't want to falsely accuse him of anything. Annettee knew that if her son had gone back to his bad habits with drugs, confronting the issue alone would not be easy.

While she wasn't entirely sure what the support group could do for her, she did know it could possibly provide some support from other parents. "So, there I was, and my turn had come to speak. Ignoring the butterflies in my stomach, I simply said, 'I am here for some support to confront my son.' And I explained how I was still waiting for some clear evidence."

As the meeting progressed Annettee did her best to turn off her issue and be attentive to the others as they shared. Soon, another woman only two seats away from Annettee was sharing her story. It was similar to Annettee's. The woman had caught her son on the phone speaking to someone who could help him acquire drugs. She said. "If I ever meet . . ."

As soon as the name was spoken, Annettee spoke out in amazement, "That's my son!" The whole group gasped. Says Annettee, "I now had my proof. God had chosen this route to answer my prayer."

The very next day Annettee firmly, but lovingly, shared what she had learned with her son Tim. He realized that he was caught in the act and did not try to deny his involvement with drugs. Annettee says that it was a bittersweet moment for her. She was relieved that Tim confessed his problem and was willing to go for help, and yet she was saddened by the fact that her suspicion had proven to be a reality. But she stayed focused that God was faithful to answer her prayer; holding on to that gave her hope for Tim's recovery.

The next day, Annettee and Tim sought out help at a drug treatment center that was close to their home. They found the counselors very helpful and easy to talk with. This made them both feel somewhat at ease.

As they met with the counselors, a problem soon arose: Tim refused to stay at the facility. He walked out the door and headed for the car. They couldn't *make* him stay—he had to be willing to accept treatment. Annettee could tell that it was going to take great willpower and faithfulness on her son's part to overcome this enemy.

With some prayer and tender, loving coaxing, Annettee persuaded Tim to go back inside the treatment center. With determination and understanding, the counselors helped Tim settle down and agree on outpatient treatment. The calm tone in his voice reassured Annettee that her son would agree to this option.

The treatment program selected for Tim required him to attend meetings three times a week for several months. Some of the meetings required Annettee's attendance as well. She and Tim sat in these group meetings with other youths and their parents to discuss any relationship or emotional issues they were encountering. Annettee felt uneasy at times when arguments burst out between parents and children. The tense arguments often resulted in explosions of anger and rage. Often, parents or their children stormed out of the room. But Annettee was relieved because Tim was always respectful to her. She was also amazed at Tim's honesty and openness as he discussed the details of buying, using, and selling drugs.

During the course of treatment, Annettee saw many of the group members give up and drop out of the program. Each day, as it drew close to their time to leave for the treatment center, Annettee would get anxious, wondering if Tim would be home in time to make it. Her faith in God, and her admiration for Tim's persistence, grew as Tim never missed a meeting.

Annettee watched as Tim found new acquaintances and the mysterious daily phone calls faded into the past. Tim successfully beat his drug problem. Today, Tim is a mature responsible father of two children, and has a stable job and a changed life.

Annettee has learned to stay persistent in prayer and to rely on God's help with all her needs. She never returned to another Tough Love meeting. But she remains in awe and wonder at how God directed her there for her answer. Whenever Annettee recalls that night at that meeting, Luke 5:26 comes to mind: "We have seen wonderful and strange and incredible and unthinkable things today!" (Amplified).

In January 1980, Sybil Clark's Aunt Joey was admitted to the hospital. She was near death, having struggled with Raynaud's syndrome for the last few decades.

"After getting the call about my aunt, I immediately began to pray," says Sybil. "I knew my aunt wasn't a Christian, and I feared for her soul. I called all of the Christian people I knew at the time and asked them to pray for her. My prayer was that, before she dies, someone, anyone, would come to her in the hospital and offer her the Lord Jesus Christ. I absolutely trusted that the Father would answer my prayer and send someone to her, even if it was a complete stranger walking down the hall at the hospital.

She didn't die as quickly as they thought she would. She kept hanging on."

In Aunt Joey's final days she was, to put it lightly, a miserable soul. She was very bitter and verbally vicious to people. She was in terrible pain, knew she was dying, and wasn't leaving this world contented.

Sybil called her mom regularly to ask about Aunt Joey. She was in the hospital throughout January and then she was discharged to go home and finish her life. There was nothing else medical science could do for her. She was heavily medicated for pain. Sybil continued to pray that someone would get to her aunt and offer her the Lord Jesus Christ before she died. Aunt Joey continued to live, week after week, month after month, against all odds.

In April, during a break from school, Sybil visited her mother in Victoria, British Columbia, where Aunt Joey also lived. Caught up with other activities during her short stay, it was the last night before she returned to college when Sybil realized she had not yet visited Aunt Joey.

"I felt terrible," says Sybil. "I was driving home from a meeting when I realized I hadn't gotten over to see her. In the darkness, I became confused on my way home that night. I was quite frustrated. I finally came to a four-way stop. I looked up at the sign and it said Blenkensop Street. I was totally stunned. My aunt's house was just a block off of this street. I realized the Lord had directed my path. At that moment, I knew that the person I asked the Lord for was me. I just knew He had preserved her life until I was able to come to Victoria so that I could be the one that led Aunt Joey to the Lord."

Sybil pulled up to her aunt's house. Her uncle, who was against all things religious, wasn't home that night. Because Aunt Joey was too weak to get out of bed, the front door was left unlocked all the time, so people could let themselves in. Sybil went in and found Aunt Joey in her bedroom. Aunt Joey greeted her niece warmly. She had been reading a Bible. Sybil's uncle wouldn't let his wife pray or read the Bible, so she was hiding it from him. Says Sybil, "She then went on to tell me that while she was in the hospital in January she had a life-after-death experience. She said that at the moment she died she was no longer in pain. Her body felt wonderful, for the first time in her life. She was at peace. She said she saw a bright light ahead but she was unable to go toward it. She wanted to stay in that place because it was so serene, so wonderful. She was angry when she came to, in pain, still alive, in the hospital. Interestingly, what I had been told about her temperament was completely opposite to how she was when I was there."

Since that day in the hospital, Aunt Joey had been reading a Bible and watching Christian programs on the television when her husband wasn't at home. Sybil told her aunt that God had allowed her a glimpse of glory, and now she had an opportunity to accept Christ as her Savior so she could go to heaven forever. Aunt Joey was eager to know how she might do this.

"We prayed together," says Sybil. "I led her through the sinner's prayer and she prayed and asked the Lord Jesus into her life. Aunt Joey told me she wasn't afraid of death because she knew what it would be like and she was happy to go and be there. She was so happy, so contented. We shared a beautiful moment of joy together."

The next day Sybil left to start a study-travel tour of the Holy Land. About two weeks later, while she was in Greece, Sybil called her mother and asked how Aunt Joey was. Her mother said Aunt Joey was just fine, but the tone in her mother's voice told Sybil that was not the case. After Sybil returned, her mother told her the truth—Aunt Joey had died a week after Sybil had left. Aunt Joey never told anyone about her experience in the hospital or about Sybil's visit. However, the night she died, her son dreamed that he saw his mom enter a white light.

Some time later, while talking with her mother again, her mother shared how all the relatives were feeling so bad that she died so bitter and miserable. Sybil then told her mother of her visit with Aunt Joey. "I told mom Aunt Joey was completely at peace when she died. My mom was relieved to know that her sister had died in peace." Sybil's mother shared the news with the relatives. All were surprised but happy for the miracle of peace and contentment that Aunt Joey finally received at the end of her life.

In August 1986, on the heels of an unwanted divorce, Stephen Clark packed all he owned into the back of a small U-Haul truck, said a tearful goodbye to his young son, and headed to New Jersey and the only job he had been able to land. He would be working for a small Christian book publishing company in South Plainfield.

Stephen had never been farther east than Ohio and knew no one in New Jersey. He drove straight through the night and checked into a motel across the highway from his new place of employment.

"I had no idea what to expect since I was hired over the phone. I needed to get oriented, find an affordable place to live, unload the truck, and return it—all within three days."

Stephen picked up a paper the next morning, checked for apartments in the classifieds, and went into his new office. "Everyone was really friendly and very welcoming. I let them know I was looking for a place to live and showed them a few places I could afford listed in the paper. I was told that each one was located in a potentially unsafe area, which was why they were so affordable."

Stephen told his dilemma to Ray, a coworker. He wanted to at least find some place temporary to live rather than be stuck in a motel. Ray had some friends with an attic apartment for rent. He gave them a call and they invited Stephen and Ray over for dinner.

John and Marie Lent were two of the nicest people Stephen had ever met. They readily welcomed him into their home. Both were committed Christians, and John was blind. As they ate dinner, Stephen shared his need for a place to live. As it turned out, their extra apartment was already spoken for.

The next day, back in the office, Stephen continued perusing the classifieds and making phone calls. In spite of the warnings from his coworkers, he made appointments to see several apartments in seedy areas—he needed a place to live soon because he had to return the rental truck.

Around mid-afternoon, just before Stephen was going to head out to look at apartments, he received a call from

John Lent: "Stephen, good news! It turns out that the girl we promised the apartment to had signed a lease with some girlfriends before talking to us. She thought she could get out of that lease, but it turns out she can't. So, if you're interested, we'd love to have you as a renter!"

Without hesitation, Stephen took the apartment and told John he'd be over right away to unload his belongings. Having seen the size of the apartment the night before, Stephen knew he wouldn't be able to get everything he had into it. So he grabbed Ray, pulled the truck around to the back of the building, and selectively removed items, mostly boxes of books, for storage in the warehouse.

Then he and Ray headed over to the Lents' where they unloaded the rest of the truck. "We had to carry everything up a narrow stairway in the house and maneuver a tight corner. Fortunately I didn't own any real furniture, just a desk, a dresser, a television, and so on, so it wasn't too challenging. Still, it took us several minutes."

And every minute counted—the cutoff time for delivering the truck without incurring a hefty penalty was 6:00 P.M. As soon as the truck was empty, Ray and Stephen headed to the nearest U-Haul dealership in rush-hour traffic. They arrived and Stephen walked up to the door just as the owner was locking it for the night. "I not only avoided the late fee, but in looking over the paperwork, the man found an error and said I'd get a refund!"

That night, Stephen was warmly welcomed into his new home. John and Marie treated him just like family. Both had been through painful divorces themselves, and they were able to minister to Stephen's pain. They also freely provided a standing invitation to evening meals. After he had headed up for the night, someone knocked on his door.

Stephen opened it to find John standing on the steps holding a roll of toilet paper and a bar of soap. "Marie thought you might need these since you've not had time to go shopping yet."

As it turned out, these were only the first of many miracles Stephen would experience while living in New Jersey, where he lived, in the same attic apartment, for ten years.

Getting to work was proving to be a challenge as Stephen had arrived in New Jersey without a car. But he did have a ten-speed bicycle. So, every morning, he pedaled more than five miles to and from work. His goal was to save up enough money to eventually buy a used car.

Fortunately, a drugstore, a barber, a doctor, and a couple of convenience stores were all located within easy walking distance. But for serious shopping, he had to hit the road. Grocery and clothing stores were a few miles away.

"Going shopping was an adventure, and juggling bags on the way home, a challenge," he says, now laughing about the ordeal.

One cold, windy fall day, a bicycle tire blew as Stephen was on the way to the store. Though he was still several blocks away, he decided the store was closer than his apartment, so he started walking the bike there. He was hoping to buy a patch kit to repair his bike.

Suddenly, a man on a bike appeared beside Stephen. The man didn't speak English. "From his gestures, I realized he wanted to fix my tire. He motioned me to stand back and then went to work applying a patch and using a hand pump to fill the tire."

Stephen was dumfounded and felt helpless and grateful as the man flipped the bike over onto its handlebars and expertly patched and pumped up the tire. He was as efficient as a crew member in the pits of the Indy 500. When he was done, he righted the bike, smiled, and placed the handlebars in Stephen's hands.

"When he finished I offered him money. He refused, hopped on his bike, and was gone. Was he an angel? On that cold, windy fall day, he was mine!"

As fall passed into winter and the weather was cold and wet more often than not, the bicycle grew to be far from adequate. Two coworkers who passed near Stephen's home offered to alternate giving him a ride to and from work.

Stephen was grateful, but knew he needed to get a car. The costs from his divorce had tapped him dry. He was making just enough to cover his rent and food and stay on top of payments for joint marital debts, as well as cover child support. Putting anything at all aside was tough. Stephen prayed daily for guidance and a car.

As it turned out, a man at work named Henry had acquired an old beat-up Volkswagen Beetle. The car had had a rough life, and it was clear it had even been in a few accidents. Still, the car was repairable, and Henry, an amateur mechanic, was doing just that. He planned to fix it up and sell it for a bit of a profit. As he became more fully aware of Stephen's situation, they talked about Stephen buying it. The only way Stephen could do it would be to make small payments over time.

One day, Henry said, "How about this. I'll sell you the car for only $125, and you can pay me $25 a week for five weeks." Stephen was stunned speechless, but managed to quickly agree to the deal before Henry changed his mind.

"I'd actually always wanted a Beetle. That was the most fun car to drive. And it was the only car that I could figure out how to service on my own. It served me well for about two years." After a couple of years, and a few more repairs, the little VW finally breathed its last.

Stephen began putting out the word that he needed a new car. He had made several new friends at church and in the area. Zandy, a counselor Stephen was seeing at his church, asked him what he was looking for and how much he was able to spend. Finances were still tight, so of course Stephen couldn't afford much. Zandy told him that he knew of a car that might be available, but he'd have to make a call the next day. A day or so later, Zandy had managed to find for Stephen a 1972 Plymouth Volare with leather interior and a power sunroof—for only $150. They arranged to meet at the owner's shop.

"The owner had used the car mostly on weekends to take the family to the shore," says Stephen. "He had just tired of it and left it sitting outside his shop. It hadn't been driven in over a year, but amazingly, it started on the first try."

This second car also lasted only a couple of years. "If I were a mechanic, I could have kept driving it. It was repairable, but I didn't have the time or money to deal with it. As it turned out, I was able to sell it to a high school student with the needed mechanic skills for the same price I paid for it."

Stephen's next car was another used one, but nicer, newer, and a bit more expensive. "Still," says Stephen, "it held up for only a couple of years. I decided it was time to buy a brand-new car. My financial situation had improved, but the divorce had messed up my credit history. Still,

I found a dealer that worked with me and I was able to purchase a really nice station wagon. It was great driving a new car!"

These were not the only miracles that Stephen experienced while living in New Jersey. While he was still carless, his friend Mary invited him to visit a church with her. She had heard from a friend of a church in nearby Scotch Plains and wanted to check it out. They went and, despite not knowing anyone, Stephen really felt comfortable. As soon as he acquired his VW, he began attending Evangel Church regularly, and he also became very involved in a growing singles group.

"I'd only been to the church a couple of Sundays," says Stephen. "As far as I was aware, I didn't know anyone in the entire state, let alone in the area, or in the church— I was wrong!" One day, as Stephen entered the church from the parking lot, he noticed a face that stood out from the normal crowd of 1,400 people.

"We both spotted each other at the exact same moment. I pointed to her, she pointed to me, and we both exclaimed, 'I know you!'" Stephen and the woman had been in the same class and had been friendly acquaintances at Evangel College years before. "Andrea gave me a big hug, and we quickly caught each other up as best we could before service started. She insisted I sit with her and after church introduced me to everyone she could corner. Thanks to her, I was able to quickly and painlessly get settled into the church."

After just a few years, the job for which Stephen had moved to New Jersey ended. The circumstances were complicated and drawn out as the little publishing company fell apart. Though the situation seemed very grim at first, it actually set up more fortunate situations for Stephen.

"Despite my sending out dozens of resumes and going on several job interviews, nothing was jelling. What money I had was dwindling fast, and my fridge was pretty empty. I felt like I was teetering on the brink of homelessness.

"One day, I was on the train heading into New York City for yet another interview. At one of the stops along the way, Jack, the singles pastor from the church I attended, got on. He worked in the city and was taking one of his daughters in for the day as well."

"We sat together and chatted. In Grand Central Station, as we parted, Jack grabbed my hand, said 'God bless you, brother!' and took off. Slowly I realized that I was holding something. I looked at my hand and there was money. Near tears, I refolded the three twenty-dollar bills and put them in my pocket. I could eat."

Just before Stephen lost his job, the church singles group decided to take a one-week missions trip to Mexico. Stephen had made the commitment to be included. "Despite being jobless, I knew, somehow, I would still make the trip."

Stephen had already paid part of the money needed prior to the job loss. Then, John and Marie helped pay more of the way and even waived a month's rent. "On top of that, our singles group pastor let me know someone in the congregation had paid all the rest."

It was one of two trips Stephen made to Mexico over two years. "When the idea was first brought up, I'd asked a friend, 'Do you think it's God's will for me to go?' Her reply was stunning: 'How could it not be God's will?'"

As Stephen continued job-hunting before his Mexico trip, a friend told him of a temporary position at a global telecommunications company. The company needed people with editorial experience. Stephen's friend, Craig, worked in a bid and proposal group, putting together large proposal documents.

"I was able to start work a few weeks before leaving on the Mexico trip, and continued looking for a permanent position. My immediate supervisor, Rick, and the department head, Marvin, were both understanding of my situation and let me take off for interviews as needed, as well as taking off the week to go to Mexico."

A few weeks after returning from Mexico, Rick approached Stephen. "We like the work you're doing for us," he explained. "If you're interested, I would like to bring you on as a permanent employee." Stephen was stunned and grateful, but hesitant. The truth was that he really didn't care too much for the job thus far. Plus, he had at least one more interview already lined up with CBN in Virginia. He told Rick he at least wanted to wait until after the interview to make a decision. Rick was fine with that.

"I really thought the job at CBN was 'the one.' However, it was really odd. As soon as the plane landed in Virginia Beach, I had this sense that I would end up at the telecom company. The interview went well, and I met a lot of people throughout the day, but by the time I got back to New Jersey, I knew what my decision was supposed to be.

"Still, I stalled. In my heart I didn't want to work for such a huge global corporation—I felt so out of place! I kept putting Rick off while I wrestled with the Lord over the decision."

After a few days, knowing Rick was waiting for an answer and couldn't wait forever, Stephen conceded to what he knew was God's direction. He wrote a letter to CBN asking to be withdrawn from consideration for the position there and told Rick he would accept the position they were offering.

"The very next day when I went to work, the telecom company announced a corporate-wide hiring freeze. I got in just under the wire. And once I resolved myself to being there, it turned out to be a really great experience. I met some wonderful people from all over the world, was stretched personally and professionally, won a special recognition that included a trip to San Francisco, and even got to travel to Hong Kong to work on a proposal there.

"My time in New Jersey started in the midst of pain," says Stephen. "But over and over again, through small miracles and big ones, God reaffirmed His love for me. And I learned the truth of Romans 8:28, which states, 'And we know that God causes everything to work together for the good of those who love God and are called according to his purpose for them'" (NIV).

The miracles Stephen experienced in New Jersey were only a fraction of those he has experienced throughout his life, even up to the present day.

One of the brightest high-lights of Gloria MacRae's life occurred in a remote mountain city in Bolivia, South America's poorest nation. She was visiting two clinics that had been named after her—Clinica Gloria I and Clinica Gloria II. She still feels a sense of disbelief that she, seventy-six-year-old Gloria MacRae from St. Paul, Minnesota, should deserve the heartfelt words of the Bolivian doctor in charge. "Señora Gloria," he had said as his eyes clouded with emotion, "Thank you for helping so that those in need in my country are able to smile."

In her heart, Gloria doesn't feel that she deserves the honor of these clinics bearing her name. She wishes the signs on their walls could include all of the people who contributed in so many ways to make those medical facilities a reality. But the complete list of the God-loving, people-loving volunteers who built them and keep them functioning in such blessedly helpful ways would overflow her address book.

Mano a mano is a Spanish phrase that means "hand-to-hand." Gloria's friend, Joan Velasquez, and her husband, Segundo, started Mano a Mano Medical Resources in 1994 as a nonprofit volunteer organization dedicated to bringing health care and public health education to impoverished Bolivian communities.

When people ask Gloria how she became involved in the undertaking, she replies, "First I gave them $25 to help the organization get off the ground; then it took over my life."

Actually, her life was taken over when two very real miracles occurred. The first became evident when good friends insisted on throwing a party to celebrate her seventieth birthday. Although Gloria was deeply touched, she urged them not to bring gifts, and they agreed. But they knew how involved she had become in Mano a Mano. And so, unbeknownst to her, they asked each person who'd been invited to make a donation to that organization.

She was astonished when they presented her with a check for $3,500—an incredible sum for people who generally gave "sensible" gifts. Then a second miracle appeared out of the blue when an anonymous donor added another $5,000! Those sums were enough to build both clinics.

So that's how two medical clinics bear the name of Gloria MacRae, a woman who started school at the age of five in Empress, Alberta, a town that appears as a dot on the Canadian prairie. She sang in church choirs as a child and managed to be active in her church—usually a Congregational church—throughout her life and wherever she lived.

Although she was educated in a four-room school that served all twelve grades, (and was the sole graduate of her class in 1943) she went on to earn an undergraduate degree in bacteriology. Yet her interests were divided between science and human services. After moving to Minnesota, she earned a master's of social work degree in 1963. And now, her involvement with Mano a Mano satisfies both her humanitarian and medical inclinations.

"Once I retired from my career as a social worker," she explains," I had more time to devote to my favorite activity. My current job title is Chief Scrounger. But really, I don't have to scrounge. It seems that wherever I go, I'm generously offered crutches, walkers, and even wheelchairs."

The organization salvages what would otherwise go to waste. For instance, 100,000 pounds of supplies and equipment that were surplus in the United States have filled requests for medical items from struggling health care programs throughout Bolivia.

"People ask how supplies and medical equipment can possibly be transported from the states to Bolivia," she says, "and the answer demonstrates an incredible amount of cooperation. Forty-foot containers are loaded with supplies and sent by truck to New York, by ocean freighter to Arica, Chile, and by rail to La Paz, Bolivia, where volunteers unpack and prepare the items for distribution."

And who pays for these services?

"All transport is funded through the Agency for International Development," she explains.

Mano a Mano has no paid staff in the United States, but well over 100 American volunteers have contributed more than 40,000 hours in the past ten years. In Bolivia, the organization has an equal number of volunteers whose donated time even includes the specialized skills and equipment needed to airlift patients to city hospitals.

Beyond donating services, Mano a Mano employs qualified Bolivian medical staff, trains and employs Bolivian carpenters, and trains *promotores* to teach public health, perform first aid, and inform local residents about the available services.

"When I had to leave those clinics that bore my name," Gloria said, "I thought of my childhood in Alberta, Canada." Then she smiled. "I grew up in a tiny town of 300 souls. My parents owned a general store and I bagged sugar, cut wedges of cheese from huge wheels, hooked things down from high shelves with a pole. I did the bookkeeping at an old roll-top desk, and when I got my driver's license, I made all the deliveries."

Gloria still fills in for all sorts of jobs at Mano a Mano. She even makes deliveries. But now, she transports donated medical supplies in the trunk of her car.

"Yes, glancing back at the people gathered in front of the clinic to say goodbye, I had a warm sense of achievement. I truly felt fulfilled because I knew that my parents would be proud. They, too, would be grateful for the miracles that allowed me to contribute and participate in this blessed organization. I recalled a phrase my mother had often quoted when I left Bolivia. It was a saying of Horace Mann's. "To pity distress is but human; to relieve it is Godlike."

Gloria was awarded second place as Volunteer of the Year during the Minneapolis Women's Expo in January, 2003. Selected from hundreds of nominations, her name has become a synonym for dedication and inspiration. Volunteers often say that they have "gloria" in common.

—by Gloria MacRae as told to Eleanor Roth